THE IMPOSSIBLE MOURNING
OF JACQUES DERRIDA

THE IMPOSSIBLE MOURNING OF JACQUES DERRIDA

Sean Gaston

continuum
LONDON • NEW YORK

Continuum

The Tower Building
11 York Road
London SE1 7NX

80 Maiden Lane
Suite 704
New York, NY 10038

www.continuumbooks.com

British Library Cataloguing-in-Publication Data
A catalogue record for this book is available from the British Library.

ISBN 0–8264–9035–2

Library of Congress Cataloging-in-Publication Data
A catalog record for this book is available from the Library of Congress.

Typeset by RefineCatch Limited, Bungay, Suffolk
Printed and bound in Great Britain by
MPG Books Ltd, Cornwall

Contents

Écarts: Derrida and the Gap

The Impossible Mourning of Jacques Derrida was written in the first two months after the death of Jacques Derrida. How does one respond to the death of Jacques Derrida? How does one mourn for Derrida, who warned of the dangers of mourning (as idealization and interiorization), while insisting that mourning is both unavoidable *and* impossible? The *gap* that the death of Jacques Derrida has left behind is open, gaping: it cannot be closed. One can perhaps only respond by tracing the gaps (*écarts*, *béances*, *décalages*), the histories of the gap, in Derrida's work.

Plato and Hegel always recognized the importance of *the* gap: they invoke the gap (the opening, the separation, the division) and they put it to work. The inescapable gaps that *cannot* be bridged, that *cannot* be filled, play a central role in Derrida's thought and in our response to his death. The gaps in Derrida's work resist *the* gap; they swerve, deviate and wander (*écarter*) – gaps *move*. When someone or something takes *pre-cedence* (goes first, goes before, goes on ahead *and gives up its place*) a gap is opened. There (are) only gaps, the gaps that Jacques Derrida has left behind him *and* in front of him: the pre-cedence of gaps.

This tracing of gaps (*écarts*) is a preface to an *impossible* mourning, a mourning that one must *at once* avoid and affirm. It keeps returning to Derrida's *Dissemination* (1972) as a preface to *Glas* (1974), Derrida's first extended work on mourning. Gaps move, swerve and deviate and in tracing the *écarts* in Derrida's work there are unavoidable digressions on Plato (the *Cratylus*, the *Sophist*) and Hegel (the *Lectures on the History of Philosophy*) as well as on Descartes, Kant, Husserl, Heidegger, Lévinas and Lyotard. The question of how one avoids a memorial becoming a *monument* concerns the importance not only of "literature", but also of "history" in Derrida's thought. In the strange suspensions *of* literature, where the part is always greater than the whole, the gap moves, even dances. For Derrida, history (is) *the history of the departures from totality* – a history of gaps that move.

In tracing the *écarts* in Derrida's work, there is also an improbable 'history' of gaps, of *digressions* on the gap, that include: Abraham and the speeds of hospitality; the Athenians and other barbarians in classical Greece; philosophy and translation in the seventeenth century; yearning (*Sehnsucht*) in the eighteenth century; imaginative sympathy in the nineteenth century; writing and raving, and the hiding of the face of God in the twentieth century. These digressions, these histories of the gap, reiterate that *we are always trying to close the gap*. Gaps move *and* we are always trying to close the gap.

The Impossible Mourning of Jacques Derrida was written from 12 October 2004, the day of Jacques Derrida's funeral, to 17 December 2004. As with many of Derrida's works, most notably 'Envois' in *The Post Card* (1980), it is written *with* the date. It is a work of fifty-two days, with all the gaps, all the unforeseeable demands and daily events, all the finitude of *today*. Today, we are trying to close the gap that cannot be closed: the gaps of today, of *12 October 2004*.

Today (this very day, the day I am writing this) is also always *another* today (any day, the day that you are reading this) and these fifty-two days were revised in May–July 2005, with some additional deviations, swerves, *écarts*.

15 July 2005

1
The Precedant (12–29 October 2004)

12 October 2004. I shall now try and write in the past tense. Late last year a friend sent me a copy of Derrida's *Chaque fois unique, la fin du monde*, the expanded French edition of *The Work of Mourning*. Knowing since last September that Derrida was gravely ill, I could not open it. Yesterday, I sat in a café in Oxford and I began to read the first few pages. But I found that I could not read Derrida writing of those who have died, *always too soon*. As I closed the book I came across Derrida's last letter to me, dated 21 November 2003, which I had forgotten was at the back of *Chaque fois unique*. As I stared at the envelope with Derrida's signature on the upper left-hand corner and at my own name and address in his handwriting, and read the short gracious letter again, I thought what I am feeling now – reading the *traces* of one who has just died – this was what Derrida meant by *writing*. I never understood this, this terrible *Unheimlichkeit*, until now. There and not there. Still here and, already, not here: now here and nowhere. Writing is always like this. I have only just begun to understand, and it is already too late.

How does one mourn for Jacques Derrida?

Don't read him writing on the death of others. One cannot avoid thinking: is this how Derrida would like, would expect, would *anticipate*, his own funeral oration, his own memorial, to be written? Who will read at his grave, who will add the last address to *Chaque fois unique*? Will it be Jean-Luc Nancy or Hélène Cixous? Philosophy *or* literature? More than one, no more one, above all (*plus d'un, avant tout*).

Don't talk too much about yourself. About how you first saw Derrida at La Coupole in Paris on 15 March 1991 at the launch of the book *Jacques*

Derrida and how he appeared, suddenly, looking anxiously at his watch and then, like the White Rabbit, disappeared down a staircase.

Don't look for 8–9 October in that book of writing *with* dates, *The Post Card*.

Don't make too much of his own "last words" in the interview in *Le Monde* on 19 August 2004. Try to avoid anything to do with *survivre* (surviving, living on, living over), of 'surviving in dying, of *sur-vivre* before and beyond the opposition between living and dying' ('Poétique et politique de témoignage' 522). In this last interview, Derrida says *la survie* 'constitutes the very structure of what we call existence, *Da-sein*, if you like'. It is 'the most intense possible life' ('Je suis en guerre contre moi-même' 13). Yes, yes . . . but this is too hard, too much like a new understanding of writing that leaves you in tears, always.

I put the letter away, back into *Chaque fois unique*, and I closed the book. All I could think of was that I must read and that the only book that I could read was *Glas*. Because it will tell you how not to *monu-memorialize*, to idealize and interiorize the 'father' as an act of mourning, to make a monument out of a memorial, to make an *Aufhebung* of the death of Jacques Derrida (*Glas* 1b).

How does one mourn for Jacques Derrida? How does one mourn otherwise for Jacques Derrida, who has spent thirty years (from the publication of *Glas*, from 1974–2004) warning against the dangers of mourning? For Derrida, mourning (*le deuil*) is inescapable, dangerous – and impossible. Mourning always *risks* a 'narcissistic pathos', a 'reappropriation' and cannibalistic 'consumption of the other' (*The Work of Mourning* 168, 159, 225). But it also announces an 'interminable', 'inconsolable', and 'irreconcilable' *finitude* (142–3). As Derrida says in an interview from 1990:

> Even before the death of the other, the inscription in me of her or his mortality constitutes me. I mourn therefore I am [*Je suis endeuillé donc je suis*], I am – dead from the death of the other [*Je suis – mort de la mort de l'autre*], my relation to myself is first of all plunged into mourning, a mourning that is moreover impossible [*d'abord endeuillé, d'un deuil d'ailleurs impossible*]. This is what I also call the ex-appropriation, the appropriation caught in a *double bind*: I must and I must not take the other into myself [*prendre l'autre en moi*]; mourning is an unfaithful fidelity if it succeeds in interiorizing the other ideally in me, that is, in not respecting his or her infinite exteriority. ('Istrice 2. Ick bünn all hier' 321; 331)

How does one mourn *after* Derrida? I have just had an email from

Nicholas Royle, who has written eloquently of what it means to be *after* Derrida, saying that Jacques Derrida's funeral is *today*, and *today* I am going to try and write in the past tense, to keep writing.

Start with the gaps.

At the end of the beginning, in the last sentences of his first paper on Husserl, ' "Genesis and structure" and phenomenology' (1959), Derrida raises the 'historico-semantic question' of what 'precedes [*précède*] the transcendental reduction'. The transcendental reduction is 'the free act of the question, which frees itself [*s'arrache*] from the totality of what precedes [*précède*] it in order to be able to gain access to this totality' (167; 251). How does one ask about what *precedes* that which *frees itself* from everything that *precedes* it?

'The science of pure possibilities', Husserl had insisted, 'must everywhere precede the science of real facts' (*Ideas I* [1931 Preface] 7). Before Husserl, Kant had argued 'there must be a condition that precedes [*vorhergeht*] all experience and makes the latter itself possible' (*Critique of Pure Reason* [1781] 232; 168). For Kant, without such an *absolute precedence*, there can be no pure understanding, no categories, no transcendental imagination – and no transcendental philosophy. After Kant, Hegel would accept that religion 'precedes [*vorangeht*]' philosophy, but *only* so philosophy can exclude it and can *begin without it* (*Lectures on the History of Philosophy* I: 61; 82).

Already, in 1959, Derrida was preoccupied with the prefix *pre-*, with what comes before, in front, in advance. Much of his work could be described as a remarkable preoccupation with *le pre-* and *le re-*. Precede, *praecedre*, *précéder*: to come before, to go before, to travel ahead of. To precede suggests *both* to go before, to take precedence, to be first *and* to give way, to cede or to yield one's place. To *pre-cede*: going ahead, going before, *taking one's place* at the front and, at the same time, *giving up one's place* as one goes ahead.

For Derrida, it is impossible to ask Husserlian phenomenology about what *precedes* that which *frees itself* from everything that *precedes* it, about that which takes precedence without *yielding* its place:

> The question of the possibility of the transcendental reduction cannot expect an answer. It is the question of the possibility of the question, opening itself, the gap [*l'ouverture elle–même, la béance*] on whose basis the *transcendental I*, which Husserl was tempted to call "eternal" (which in his thought, in any

> event, means neither infinite nor ahistorical, quite the contrary) is called upon to ask itself about everything, and particularly about the possibility of the unformed and naked factuality of the nonmeaning, in the case at hand, for example, of its own death. (167–8; 251)

The impossible question for phenomenology of that which is *not* free to precede what it precedes is also a question of death. Derrida describes this 'question of the possibility of the question', this question for the '*transcendental I* . . . of its own death [*de sa propre mort*]', as 'opening itself, the gap [*l'ouverture elle–même, la béance*]'. Alan Bass has translated *la béance* as 'the gap', and one could also translate it as 'gaping', as the *gaping*, open wound. It is this gaping opening, 'opening itself', that raises the impossible question, the question *of* the impossible, of the *precedant* that comes *and* goes first, that *gives up its place* as it takes precedence. The *precedant* always predeceases, goes on ahead.

13 October 2004.   Start with the gaps. Five years later in his first essay on Edmond Jabès (1964), Derrida turns to another kind of gap, a Latin gap; to an interval, a break, that slips and falls:

> The other originally collaborates with meaning. There is an essential *lapse* [un lapsus] between significations which is not the simple and the positive fraudulence of a word, nor even the nocturnal memory of all language. . . . The caesura [*la césure*] does not simply finish and fix meaning . . . primarily, the caesura makes meaning emerge. It does not do so alone, of course; but without interruption – between letters, words, sentences, books – no signification could be awakened. ('Edmond Jabès and the question of the book' 71; 107–8)

These Latin gaps are the very possibility of meaning, of signification. If the gap is filled or *bridged* there is no meaning, no signification. The gap is indispensable, unavoidable: it must not be bridged. But when it comes to the gap, there is always the question of a bridge.

As Derrida notes in *The Problem of Genesis* (1953–1954), 'Hume remains the most revolutionary European philosopher for Husserl' (175). For Hume, the limitations of an understanding founded on external sense-impressions lead to an inevitable reliance on fictions of the imagination to ensure the coherence and *continuity* of perception (*A Treatise of Human Nature* 193). At the outset, from the start, at the origin, there are gaps in experience. Imagination fills the gaps. Hume works to bridge the gap. This empirical faculty of filling in the gaps of perception is not that different from Kant's *a priori* synthetic unity of the transcendental imagination as the possibility, the precondition, of any experience: both bridge the gap. For Kant, 'the principle of continuity' forbids 'any leap [*Absprung*] in the series of appearances ... but also any gap or cleft [*Lücke oder Kluft*] between two appearances in the sum of all empirical intuitions in space'. The *Critique of Pure Reason* abhors any Latin gaps that jump: '*in mundo non datur hiatus, non datur saltus* [in the world there is no hiatus, there is no leap]' (A 228–29/B 281–82). At the same time, as he bridges the gaps *of* experience, Kant insists on the *gap* between appearances and things in themselves. Without this gap, nothing can be universal, necessary and objectively valid. It is a gap that must not be bridged, a gap that *works* for reason. Hegel will inherit this gap of reason and *put it to work* for speculative dialectics: the gap as *Aufhebung*.

Husserl believed that Hume's *A Treatise of Human Nature* (1739–1740) 'gives the first systematic sketch of a pure phenomenology, which, though under the name of psychology, attempts to supply a philosophical transcendental philosophy' (*Ideas I* [1931 Preface] 16). Like Hume, Husserl argues that because 'the spatial shape of the physical thing can be given only in some single perspective aspect', there is always an 'inadequacy which clings to the unfolding of any series of continuously connected intuitions'. Unlike Hume, Husserl insists that this inadequate, individual intuition is only an *aspect* of a general, essential intuition – a pure essence. The gaps of experience *and* the fictions of imagination are always *invitations* to pure essence, to ideality (*Ideas I* §3–4: 48–51). As Derrida observes in *Speech and Phenomena* (1967), 'it is no accident that Hume's thought fascinated Husserl more and more. The power of pure repetition that opens up ideality and the power which liberates the imaginative reproduction of empirical perception cannot be foreign to each other; nor can their products' (55).

In *Speech and Phenomena* Derrida notes that Husserl accepts that in communication 'meaning [*le vouloir-dire*] is *always* entangled, *caught* [toujours *enchevêtré*, prise] in an indicative system' (20; 20, trans. modified). However, despite this '*de facto* necessity of entanglement', Husserl insists on 'the possibility of a rigorous distinction of essence' *between* expression and indication (20). For Derrida, this possibility – this refusal of the contamination of expression by indication – 'is purely *de jure* and phenomenological'. Husserl's 'whole analysis', he argues, 'will thus advance in this separation [*dans cet écart*] between *de facto* and *de jure* [*le fait et le droit*], existence and essence, reality and intentional function'. This gap (*écart*) is the possibility of intentionality for Husserl. It 'defines the very space of phenomenology' and 'is opened only in and through the possibility of language' (21; 21, trans. modified). There can be no meaning, no signification *without a gap*, without a gap that *cannot* be bridged. But there can also be no meaning, no signification, Derrida adds, without a gap that *cannot be put to work*. It is this gap, this '*divergence* [écart] between two kinds of signs', that haunts phenomenology (30; 32). It is 'the *divergence* [l'écart] of indicative communication and even of signification in general', Derrida writes, that 'opens the living to *différance*' (69; 77, trans. modified).

In French, the gap diverges, deviates; it is at once a noun (*écart*) and a verb (*écarter*). *Un écart*: a distance, a space, a gap, an interval, a difference, a deviation, a departure. *Faire un écart*: to swerve, to jump, to leap aside. *À l'écart*: to be out of the way, to be remote, to be on the side. *Mettre, tenir, rester à l'écart*: to keep back, to hold back, to stay in the background, to remain on the margins. *Écarter*: to move apart, to separate, to spread, to open, to dismiss, to remove, to exclude, to push aside, to set aside, to step back, to withdraw. To draw back behind the curtain: *derrière le rideau*.

14 October 2004. Today, a friend has sent me copies of *Libération* ('Derrida: l'homme déconstruit', 11 October), with a long and generous article on Derrida by Robert Maggiori, and *Le Monde* with a special supplement on Derrida organized by Jean Birnbaum (12 October). I also read today that Derrida asked that no words be read at his funeral. So, in the end, when it comes to a testament for Derrida, one does not have to choose between Nancy and Cixous, *between* philosophy and literature. An *impossible* decision. There is no final address to add to *Chaque fois unique*, and we are *left* with the impossible decision, with a decision *from* the impossible. As Cixous has written of Derrida, 'the scenarios of his travels, displacements and returns are always marked by the seal of the impossible' ('Ce corps étranjuif' 72). And it is in taking an unavoidable and agonizing *interest* in the impossible – an interest *from* the impossible – that I am *dis*-interested and taken away from my self *to* the other, *for* the other.

In *Of Grammatology* (1965–1967), Derrida writes of 'a primary gap and a primary *expatriation*' in the Platonic text. Spivak translates '*une coupure . . . premières*' as 'a primary gap', and it can also be translated as 'a first cut' (39; 59). In the *Cratylus*, Socrates had insisted on the *proper* cut, on the propriety of cutting: 'In cutting [*temnein*], for example, we do not cut as we please, and with any chance instrument; but we cut with the proper instrument only, and according to the natural [*phúsin*] process of cutting; and the natural process is right and will succeed, but any other will fail and be of no use at all' (387a). For Socrates, the proper cut is only an example to illustrate the proper *name* and the propriety of naming, when art, craft (*tekhnē*) naturally works for nature (*phusis*) (389).

For Derrida, the 'first cut' in the propriety of naming begins with Socrates and Phaedrus sitting 'under a plane tree, by the banks of the Illissus' (*Phaedrus* 227a). As they are sitting there, Socrates will ask, 'am I a monster [*thērion*]?' (230a). And Phaedrus will ask Socrates, 'do you ever cross the border?' (230a). And Socrates will say, 'now I am certain that this is not an invention of my own . . . and therefore that I have been filled through the ears, like a pitcher, from the waters of another' (235d). Monsters, crossing borders and the ear of the other: the 'first cut' of *writing*.

Speech, Derrida writes, is 'a *logos* which believes itself to be its own father': the Christ of language. Writing, 'since [as Socrates says] its "parent's help is always needed" [*Phaedrus* 275d] . . . must therefore be born out of a primary gap [*une coupure*] and a primary *expatriation*, condemning it to wandering and blindness, to mourning' (*Of Grammatology* 39; 59). How is mourning possible? Start with the gaps. Living speech would never be able to mourn the *loss* of the father, as it could not mourn the loss of *itself*, as living speech. With speech, there can be no mourning. The first cut of Western philosophy would be writing as the loss of the father. The gap as the first cut: no father. *Writing*, one has *always* lost the father.

15 October 2004. 'Turn to the *Cratylus*', Derrida advises ('Plato's pharmacy' 140).

> *Socrates*: Then the irreligious son of a religious father should be called irreligious?
> *Hermogenes*: Certainly.
> *Socrates*: He should not be called Theophilus (beloved of God) or Mnesitheus (mindful of God), or any of these names: if names [*onómata*] are correctly given, his should have an opposite meaning.
> *Hermogenes*: Certainly, Socrates. (394e)

Contrary to the thought of Protagoras, who believes that 'man is the measure of all things' and that things 'are to me as they appear to me, and that they are to you as they appear to you', Socrates begins the *Cratylus* by arguing that 'things must have their own proper and permanent essence'. Things are 'independent, and maintain to their own essence the relation prescribed by nature'. There is an original *gap* between us and 'things themselves' (386d). It is a natural gap, a gap that resists convention. It is on the *basis* of this unbridgeable gap that Socrates turns to the proper cut, to the propriety of cutting and the *proper name* (the name that is natural and true) as an instance of a 'proper instrument' (*tekhnē*) always working 'according to the natural process' (*phusis*) (387a). The proper name: *tekhnē* working for *phusis*.

As a 'proper instrument' working 'according to a natural process', naming relies on a transparent or virtual *tekhnē*, a *tekhnē* that disappears, that leaves no remainder. When *tekhnē* appears to work for *phusis*, *form* triumphs over *matter*: 'when a man has discovered the instrument which is naturally [*phúsei*] adapted to each work, he must express this natural [*phúsei*] form, and not others which he fancies, in the material, whatever it may be, which he employs . . . the form [*idéan*] must stay the same, but the material may vary' (389c, 389e–390a). Names are 'the true forms [*eidos*] of things in letters' (390a). 'The irreducible privilege of the name [*du nom*]', Derrida will write in 'The pit and the pyramid' (1968), 'is the keystone [*la clé de voûte*] of the Hegelian philosophy of language' (96; 112). It is the gap that binds Hegel to Plato.

For Derrida, *naming* is always the announcement of 'a death to come [*d'une mort à venir*]', of 'a name that survives whoever carries that name' ('The animal that therefore I am' 389; 270; Royle, *Jacques Derrida*). Naming is the inescapable beginning of mourning. 'First of all, mourning [*D'abord le deuil*]. We will be speaking of nothing else' (*Specters of Marx* 9; 30).

17 October 2004. 'The form must be the same, but the material may vary.' Socrates uses this order between form and matter to argue that when it comes to naming, 'whether in Hellas or in a foreign country; – there is no difference' (390a). There is, apparently, no gap between the Greeks and the barbarians, as long as the *philosopher* keeps the legislator, the maker of names, 'whether he be Hellene or barbarian', in order (391a). As Hegel at Jena on *13 October 1806* would see the philosopher at the end of history, Socrates sees the philosopher at the end of the name (Kojève, *Introduction to the Reading of Hegel* 35).

It is only *after* this end of the proper name that Socrates takes on (mimes) the role of the *etumologos*, a masterful student of etymology, of the *etymon*, the *true* form of words (391–421). The *etymon* begins with proper names. At the same time, as Socrates displays or performs the truth of names, everything seems to turn to Heraclitus, to perpetual motion and speeds (402). The *etymon* makes us run, rush and speed.

'You are quickening your pace now, Socrates' (420b).

From the start, this speeding appears to be inescapable. Because men first associated the gods with the stars, 'seeing that they were always moving and running, from their running nature they were called Gods or runners (*Theous, Theontas*)' (397d). Wisdom (*Phronesis, Sophia*) itself cannot escape the *etymon* of 'motion [*phoras*] and flux', or 'touching the motion or stream of things' (411–12). Socrates, criticizing a seemingly unavoidable Heraclitian-Protagorian genealogy of naming, remarks:

> I believe that the primeval givers of names were undoubtedly like too many of our modern philosophers, who, in their search after the nature of things, are always getting dizzy [*eiliggiosis*] from constantly going round and round, and then they imagine that the world is going round and round and moving in all directions; and this appearance, which arises out of their own internal condition, they suppose to be a reality of nature; they think that there is nothing stable or permanent, but only flux and motion, and that the world is always full of every sort of motion and change. (411b–c)

Hegel, Derrida notes at the beginning of *Glas*, will insist on the 'disqualification of etymology' (10a). Socrates will bring order to this dizziness of names and naming by emphasizing that the *etymon* of motion always returns to the good and that the *etymon* of the name *name* (*ónoma*) is a matter of being (*ón*). The name *name* returns us to being, to the 'search' for being (421a–b). This is where Heidegger starts. Having *already* imitated the *etumologos*, it is only *after* ending with ontology as the proper end of the proper name, of the proper cut, that Socrates turns to the problem of *mimēsis*, which Derrida will trace in 'Plato's pharmacy' (137–42) and 'The double session' (188). For Socrates, *mimēsis* always follows ontology.

Socrates argues that it is because the form is always the same while the material varies that there is 'no difference' between the Hellenes and other barbarians when it comes to the proper name. At the same time, he admits that when it comes to the *etymon*, 'names that we do not understand are of a foreign nature [*barbarikón*]' (421d). When it comes to the *gap* between the Greeks and the barbarians – a gap which Herodotus was perhaps the first to respect, opening his inquiry (*historia*), opening history, in this gap – material variations do make a difference to the search for the *etymon*. The attempt to derive the origin of Greek names from the

barbarians, who are 'older than we are', is, Socrates says, 'only an ingenious excuse for having no reason concerning the truth of words' (426a).
The barbarian: the others who pre-cede Greek naming, the others who
have, already, opened gaps in the *eytmon*. Socrates' worst anxiety is the
barbarian who imitates, who creates a copy of a thing and names it, a copy
with a form that is *not* the same: a barbarian double (432). In 'The trace of
the other' (1963), Lévinas had written, always with the walls of Athens in
mind, of 'the wild barbarian character of alterity [*la barbarie sauvage de
l'altérité*]' (345; 261–2).

20 October 2004.   A swerve, a deviation (an *écart*) on Plato (and the
gap that *launches* the proper name and the gaps that cut the propriety of
naming) that started from the translation in *Of Grammatology* of '*une
coupure . . . premières*' as 'a primary gap' in the Platonic text. Later in *Of
Grammatology*, in Derrida's reading of Rousseau, there is another translation of the gap. Derrida has turned to the question of representation. He
writes:

> What cannot be thus represented by a line is the turn (trick/trope) of the
> re-turn [*le tour du re-tour*] when it has the bearing of re-presentation. What one
> cannot represent is the relationship of representation to so-called originary
> presence. The re-presentation is also a de-presentation. It is tied to the work of
> spacing.
>   Spacing insinuates into presence an interval [*un intervalle*] which not only
> separates the different times of speech and song but also the represented from
> the representer. (203; 289)

While here Derrida links the interval to *spacing*, two pages later he links it
to *temporization*. As soon as there is representation, one cannot avoid 'the
gap [*le décalage*] between the thing and its double' (205; 291). Spivak
translates *le décalage* as the gap. *Un décalage*, a gap, an interval, is also a
time lag: the time difference (*le décalage horaire*). For Derrida, there (are)
always *gaps*: the gaps of space becoming time and of time becoming
space, the gaps *of différance* and gaps *as différance* – *différance* always leaves a
gap (262; 'Différance' 13).

In *The Post Card* (1980) on *22 September 1977* Derrida will write: 'The
time difference is in me, it is me [*Le décalage horaire est en moi, c'est moi*]'
('Envois' 108; 118).

The gap: *c'est moi*. As I finished typing *c'est moi*, the telephone rang and
she said: *c'est moi*.

21 October 2004. Today – by chance and almost two weeks after Jacques Derrida's death – I am going to Paris.

25 October 2004. In Heathrow on the Thursday afternoon the plane was delayed and while standing in front of the departures screen we began to talk to a young Frenchman who worked for the water department in Toulouse and who was also . . . Jean-Luc Nancy's nephew. He said that his uncle had been with Jacques Derrida the day before he died.

Before I went to Paris, I had thought of visiting Derrida's grave, but I had missed an email in Oxford from Nicholas Royle by a few hours and did not know where to go. Somehow it seemed very right that my act of mourning was to go to the bookshops *PuF* and *Vrin* in the Place de la Sorbonne and *La Hune* on the Boulevard Saint Germain and to buy more of Derrida's books. To keep reading. To keep writing.

In *PuF*, I opened the latest *Cahiers de l'Herne* devoted to Derrida and by chance I came across my own name, quoted, translated and endnoted for the first time in French. I was surprised by my name in the Place de la Sorbonne. It was only yesterday back in England that I discovered there had been a gathering for Derrida on Friday in Paris at the Collège international de philosophie. Both Jean-Luc Nancy and Hélène Cixous had spoken.

In an interview on *17 June 1971* Derrida said in parentheses, if one can speak in parentheses:

> Henceforth, in order better to mark this interval (*La dissémination*, the text that bears this title, since you have asked me about it, is a systematic and playful exploration of the interval – *"écart", carré, carrure, carte, charte, quatre*, etc.) it has been necessary to analyze, to set to work, *within* the text of the history of philosophy, as well as *within* the so-called literary text (for example, Mallarmé), certain marks, shall we say (I mentioned certain ones just now, there are many others), that *by analogy* (I underline) I have called undecidables. (*Positions* 42–3)

Not just the text I would add, but the "book" *La dissémination* (1968–1972), which begins: 'This (therefore) will not have been a book [*Ceci (donc) n'aura pas été un livre*]' (3; 9). I don't think Derrida has ever written a book, only articles, papers, fragments of seminars and prefaces as strategic traces of *différance*. There are prefaces everywhere: 'You might read these *envois* as the preface to a book that I have not written' ('Envois' 3); 'This essay resembles a lengthy preface. It would rather be the foreword to a book that I would one day wish to write' (*Politics of Friendship* vii). *Dissemination*: gaps, cuts, intervals and time differences, *prefaces* to *Glas*, preface to an impossible mourning on the gap, on the gaping opening that the death of Jacques Derrida has left behind.

In 'Outwork, prefacing [Hors livre: préfaces]' (1972), the opening of *Dissemination*, Derrida writes of 'the impossibility of summing up the gap at a single point or under a single name [*l'impossibilité de résumer l'écart en un seul point, voire sous un seul nom*]'. It is always a question of *écarts*, of gaps under more than one name, of gaps *in* the name, in naming, of the gaps that pre-cede the *etymon*. The gaps 'must remain open', Derrida argues, letting themselves be 'ceaselessly marked and remarked [*sans cesse marquer et remarquer*]' (6; 12). '*différance*', Derrida had insisted in his 1968 paper, 'is not announced [or preceded] by a capital letter': see page 22 of what is still translated as 'Di*ff*érance' in *Margins of Philosophy* (1982). *différance* 'cannot be preceded [*précéder*] by any identity, any unity, or any original simplicity' (6; 12). *différance* cannot be pre-ceded by *the* gap (*Positions* 8). *différance* always pre-cedes *the* gap – takes precedence and gives up its place, gives up *the* place. *différance* pre-cedes *the* gap as the destination of the place, of the proper name: *écarts*.

On *6 June 1977* one of the narrators in 'Envois' writes a postcard from Oxford:

> Be aware that everything in our bildopedic culture, in our politics of the encyclopedic, in our telecommunications of all genres, in our telematicometa-physical archives, in our library, for example the marvellous Bodleian, everything is constructed on the protocolary charter of an axiom, that could be demonstrated, displayed on a large *carte*, a post card of course, since it is so simple, elementary, a brief, fearful stereotyping (above all say or thinking nothing that derails, that jams telecom). The charter is the contract for the following, which quite stupidly one has to believe: Socrates comes *before* [avant] Plato, there is between them – and in general – an order of generations, an irreversible sequence of inheritance. Socrates is before, not in front of, but before Plato, therefore behind him [*Socrates est avant, pas devant mais avant Platon, donc derrière lui*], and the charter binds us to this order: this is how to orient one's thought, this is the left and this is the right, march. (20; 25)

But what if, as the postcard that Derrida sees in the Bodleian suggests, Plato *also* comes before, is behind, Socrates? Kant would be driven to distraction by such a mad pre-cedence, by a precedence that comes after *différance*. For Kant, the only way to escape Hume's relegation of causality

to a subjective contingency (the imagination) is through the rule of precedence, the order of the temporal sequence: 'something happens [*etwas
geschiehet*]' and 'we always presuppose that something else precedes [*etwas
vorausgehe*] it', and 'I cannot reverse the series' (*Critique of Pure Reason*
A 195/B 240, A 198/B 243). Precedence is always and only that which
comes first, comes before what follows, in time and according to a rule: it
gives causality necessity and objective validity. *Pre-cedence*, on the other
hand, indicates someone or something that could be either *before* (first) or
ahead (first), that might be at once *behind* (first) or *out in front* (first);
something or someone that comes first, goes first, and in *taking* its place
has *already* given up its place, given up *the place*. What 'precedes us [*nous
précèdent*]', Derrida remarks in *The Specters of Marx* (1993), is 'as much *in
front of us* as *before us* [*aussi bien* devant nous *qu'* avant nous]' (17; 41).

'You will always precede me [*tu me précéderas toujours*]' ('Envois' 19; 24).

26 October 2004.   'Something happens', Kant had written. 'Something
happens [*se passe*], something *takes place* [*a lieu*]', Derrida writes in 'Restitutions' (1977–1978), tracing the dispute between Meyer Schapiro and
Heidegger over Van Gogh's painting of shoes, 'when shoes are abandoned
. . . apparently detached from the feet' (265; 302). For Hegel, on the other
hand, one can forget about the problem of shoes because in the end, 'the
feet [*die Füße*] of those who will carry you out are *already* at the door'
(*Phenomenology of Spirit* 45; 67, my emphasis). In *Identity and Difference*
(1957), Heidegger had contrasted the movement of the Hegelian *Aufhebung* that already will take you out of the door to 'the step back [*der Schritt
zurück*]' (49; 115). For Derrida, it is all a question of pace, of the step (*pas*),
the rhythm of the *pas* (the not, the negative), that *neither* carries you out
(to absolute knowledge) *nor* takes you back (to difference as thinking),
but limps (*boite*) ('To speculate' 405–9; 'Pas' 34–6, 41, 48).

The *Aufhebung* of *le pré-*. For Hegel, the *pre-* of the preface is always, 'in
truth', *preceded* by the book, by what appears to be in front of it, by that
which *presents itself*, by that which keeps its *place* ('Outwork' 11; 17). The
Aufhebung of the *pre-* is 'opened up by the critical gap [*ouvert par l'écart
critique*] between the logical or scientific development of philosophy and
its empiricist or formalist lag'. For Hegel, there is always a gap. And, Derrida
adds, 'this, indeed, is a lesson of Hegel's to be maintained, if possible,
beyond Hegelianism: the essential complicity between empiricism and formalism' (11; 18). A lesson of Hegel: the gap *works* for 'the auto-production
and auto-determination of the concept' (11; 18, trans. modified).

Hegelianism: 'one must then go on to recognize the gap [*l'écart*]', the gap that *fills itself*, that makes a *place* for 'autopresentation' ('Outwork' 12, 15; 19, 22, trans. modified). But the *pre-* of the Hegelian preface *also* remains, it is not entirely effaced by what is in front of it, it leaves a *remainder* and, Derrida writes, 'its spacing (preface to a rereading) diverges [*s'écarte*] in (the) place of the χώρα [*khōra*]' (16; 24). The relation between *le pré*, the gap that diverges, deviates, differs and the question of taking, keeping or giving up a *place* takes us from a promised re-reading (the *re-* is never far away) at the opening of *Dissemination* in 1972 to Derrida's reading of Plato's *khōra* in 1987.

Derrida had first promised to come back to *khōra* in 'Plato's pharmacy' (1968) (161). Thoth, the Egyptian god of writing makes an early appearance as the Greek *khōra*: 'always taking a place [*prenant toujours la place*] which is not his own, and that one can also call the place of death [*la place du mort*], he does not have either a proper place or a proper name [*il n'a pas de lieu ni de nom propres*]' (93; 115, trans. modified). Five years later in 'Outwork' Derrida writes of the preface: 'its spacing (preface to a rereading) diverges in (the) place of the χώρα [*son espacement (préface à une relecture) s'écarte au lieu de la χώρα*]'. The spacing of the *pre-* diverges, deviates, parts, departs, withdraws (*s'écarte*) in the place, in *place of* the place (*khōra*). Nearly twenty years later, Derrida writes *Khōra* (1987–1993) and turns back to the 'mother' of all gaps – to the Platonic gaps that *remain* unfilled, unbridged and that '*give place* [donner lieu]' to a place ('*Khōra*' 90, 95 [28], 124). Gaps: the 'pre-origin' of place – '*if there is place*' (125–6, 100).

27 October 2004. 'Socrates privileges here again the situation, the relation to place' ('*Khōra*' 107). For Derrida, *khōra* '*gives* nothing in giving place [donner *rien en donnant lieu*]' (96; 30). *Khōra gives place* to place without receiving or conceiving (95). *Khōra* situates without being situated (92). It is the possibility of place that is without place: a gap. *Khōra* 'cannot be translated into absent support or into absence as support'. It 'provokes and resists any binary or dialectical determination' and cannot be reduced to the great ontological opposition of 'intelligible *or* sensible'. 'Simply', Derrida writes, 'this excess [of *khōra*] is nothing, nothing that may be and be said ontologically' (97, 99).

Khōra ' "precedes"["*précède*"]' (126; 95). Derrida's quotation marks here can be read as a gesture to a pre-cedence that comes before and goes ahead, that takes precedence and always yields its place, always gives up *the* place. With the Husserlian concept of precedence in mind (that which frees itself from everything that precedes it), Derrida often takes care to displace the presumption of place in *précéder* by putting it in quotation marks ('Plato's pharmacy' 127; *Aporias* 44). In 1987 Derrida describes *khōra* as 'a gaping opening [*une ouverture béante*]' (103; 45), an echo of his 1959 paper on Husserl and 'opening itself, the gap [*l'ouverture elle–même, la béance*]'. Gaps – *béances, coupures, intervalles, décalages, écarts* – *provoke* and *resist* the gap that fills itself, that bridges itself, that gives place to *the* place, to the place without gaps, if such a thing were possible.

La dissémination s'écarte – diverges, deviates, departs, withdraws – towards *Glas*, towards a preface to an *impossible* mourning. *Écarts*: the memorial that takes pre-cedence and *gives away* the *place* for monuments, the place for a monu-memorialization in which the dead are either *always* with us (inside us, and present) or *never* with us (outside of us, and absent). *Either* in us *or* outside of us: two places, two monuments to the dead, to the dead *either* in us (the monument as subject) *or* outside of us (the monument as object), two columns.

The pre-cedence of the place gives away the either/or.

28 October 2004.   Hegel's *écarts* appear in two footnotes in 'Outwork', in French translations from the *Lectures on the History of Philosophy* (1805–1831): ' "Thus they have the category in which they can place any apparently significant philosophy, and through which they may at any time set it aside [*écarter*]; this they call a fashion-philosophy [une philosophie *à la mode*]" ' (17 n. 19; 26 n. 12); ' "It [this introduction] must serve to set aside [*écarter*] many questions and demands which might, from our ordinary prejudices, arise in such a history" ' (18 n. 20; 27 n. 13). An *Aufhebung* of *écarts* demonstrated in footnotes. For Hegel, the setting aside (*écarter*) *of* philosophy is *already* set aside (*écarter*) *by* philosophy. Everything relies, in advance, on the *pre-*. At the same time, as Derrida comments, Hegel must renounce the primacy of the *pre-*: 'the *Logic* cannot be preceded [*précéder*] by any lemma or prolemma' (19; 28). The preface is at once before *and* after; it is the *last* word appearing as the *first* word, the last word which must not pre-empt the beginning on its journey to the end. The Hegelian *pre-*, the *anticipation* of all the gaps that can intrude along the course of the history of spirit to its end, *must not* pre-cede (take its place first *and* be the first to give up the place) or set aside (*écarter*) history *as* spirit.

The *pre-* will remain (*reste*) a remainder, a gap.

Hegelianism: 'reducing all absolute dehiscence between writing and meaning [*vouloir-dire*], by erasing a certain event of the break [*un certain événement de la coupure*] between *anticipation* and *recapitulation*' (20; 30, trans. modified). For Hegel, in the end, there is 'no more gap [*plus d'écart*] . . . only a *presentation* of the concept by itself' (30–1; 42, trans. modified). For Derrida, there is always *plus d'un* (more than one/no more one), and it is 'a certain event of the break [*la coupure*, the cut]' that decapitates Hegelianism.

The failure of *Aufhebung* of the *pre-* is marked by Derrida in the gap of the pre-face, in 'the gap [*l'écart*] between the empty "form", and the fullness of "meaning" ["*sens*"]'. This gap in Hegel's text 'is structurally irremediable, and any formalism, as well as any thematicism, will be impotent to domin- ate that structure. They will miss it [*la manquent*] in their very attempt to master it' (21; 30). It is this gap, this gaping that diverges, that dis- tinguishes *dissemination*: 'In diverging [*s'écarter*] from polysemy, compris- ing both more and less than the latter [from Ricoeur's hermeneutics of polysemy where the word – speech – *fills* the gap, *bridges* the gap, between structure and event, synchrony and diachrony, *The Conflict of Interpretations* 80, 89–95; Derrida, 'La Parole: Donner, nommer, appeler' 20], dissemin- ation interrupts the circulation that transforms an after-effect of meaning into an origin [*transforme en origine un après-coup du sens*]' (21; 30, trans. modified). In 'Signature event context' (1971), Derrida had already emphasized 'the necessity of, in a way, *separating* [*d'écarter*] the concept of polysemia from the concept I have elsewhere named dissemination' (316; 376). He concludes his 1971 paper by defining writing as 'a disseminating operation *separated* [*écartée*] from presence (of Being)' (330; 393). It is the gaps *of* and *as* dissemination that resist ontology.

But 'we have not yet finished with Hegel', Derrida warns in 'Outwork'. 'No doubt Hegel, too allows for the insistence of a certain gap [*d'un certain écart*] between the form and the content . . . [and] isn't *The Phenomenology of Spirit* precisely the history of such discrepancies [*décalages*]?' (21; 30). *The Phenomenology of Spirit*, Derrida suggests, is a history – if such a thing is possible – of *décalages*, of gaps, of time differences: an impossible history of *travelling*. Impossible because, as Catherine Malabou has observed, from Plato to Hegel 'the origin does not travel [*l'origine ne voyage pas*]' and yet, and yet, 'travel takes the origin away with it' (*Counterpath* 6–8; 14). What distinguishes the *écart* of Hegel from the *écarts* of dissemination is the *pre-* that cannot avoid the *re-*. Hegel puts the gap to work 'according to the overflow of a re-mark [*l'excès d'une re-marque*] (a preface on prefaces, a preface within a preface) of which dissemination must problematize the formal rules and the abyssal movement' (21; 31).

In the end, the preface as the gap between form and content is a matter of life and death. According to Hegel, formalism, or Schelling's philosophy of nature – or a certain view of structuralism – is a kind of death, a closed and labelled box ('Outwork' 22–4). In the preface to the second edition of the *Logic* Hegel opposes 'the life of the concept' to this death, which is *also* linked in Derrida's French translation to a certain *écart*. Hegel writes:

> What results from this method of labelling all . . . is a synoptic table like a skeleton with scraps of paper stuck all over it, or like the rows of closed and labelled boxes in a grocer's stall (*in einer Gewürzkrämerbude*). It is easy to read off as either of these; and just as all the flesh and blood has been stripped from this skeleton, and the no longer living "essence" has been packed away in the boxes (*Büchsen*), so in the report the living essence of the matter has been stripped away or boxed up dead [*un semblable tableau a écarté ou caché profondément l'essence vivante de la chose*]. (24; 34; *Science of Logic* 31)

The 'living essence of the thing [*la chose*]' has been 'separated or hidden' (*écarté ou caché*). In putting the *écart* to work, Hegel is only confronted by another *écart*: there is always more than one gap, no one gap.

29 October 2004.   A wet and cold Friday. There are twenty-seven starlings on the roof across from my window. In *Of Grammatology*, a few pages before the primary gap as a first cut in the Platonic text, there is the great passage on representation:

> Representation mingles with what it represents . . . [and] in this play of representation the point of origin becomes ungraspable . . . There is no longer a simple origin. For what is reflected is split *in itself* and not only as an addition to itself of its image. The reflection, the image, the double, splits what it doubles. The origin of the speculation becomes a difference. What can look at itself is not one [*Ce qui peut se regarder n'est pas un*]: and the law of the addition of the origin to its representation, of the thing to its image, is that the one plus one makes at least three [*un plus un font au moins trois*]. (36; 55)

Derrida returns to this first trace of his later reading of Freud ('one two three – speculation without term', 'To speculate – on "Freud" ' 283) in 'Outwork'. It is a question of squares and triangles, numbers and gaps. 'We should wait until there are even more than two of us', one of the voices says in 'Restitutions' (257).

In 'Outwork' Derrida quotes in bold a gap in quotes, a gap apparently without an author: ' "**the splayed square [***le carré écarté***] loosens up [***desserre***] the obsidionality of the triangle**" ' (25; 36). It is only some three hundred and twenty-five pages later in *Dissemination*, when reading the essay 'Dissemination' (1969), that this anonymous gap in quotes appears as a *re*-citation of Derrida himself. He writes in 'Dissemination': 'Even though it is only a triangle open on its fourth side, the splayed square [*le carré écarté*] loosens up the obsidionality of the triangle and the circle which in their ternary rhythm (Oedipus, Trinity, Dialectics) have always governed metaphysics. It loosens them up; that is, it de-limits them, reinscribes them, re-cites them [*le ré-cite*]' (352; 428).

The triangle or trinity of dialectical speculation (thesis–antithesis–synthesis) always re-turns to itself *and* oversteps itself, displaces and replaces itself in 'the excess of a re-mark [*l'excès d'une re-marque*]' ('Outwork' 21; 31, trans. modified). 'The "three" ', Derrida writes, 'will no longer give us the ideality of the speculative solution but rather the effect of a strategic re-mark [*d'une re-marque stratégique*]' (25; 35). When there is more than one gap, no one gap, when the place of death cannot be reduced to *the* place, the *re-* cannot be distinguished from the *pre-*. Dissemination displaces 'the two of binary oppositions' and the 'three of speculative dialectics' into a four (*quatre*), a square (*carré*) that is always a *re-citation*, a ' "**splayed square [***le carré écarté***]**" '. Not one gap (working *for* binary oppositions), nor two gaps (working *for* speculative dialectics): always three *or more* gaps – *écarts*. How does one mourn for Jacques Derrida? Start with the gaps.

Prefatory aside (*à l'écart préfacier*) (56; 73).

2

Histories–Décalages (1–30 November 2004)

1 November 2004. On *28 October 1816* in Heidelberg Hegel gave his inaugural address for his forthcoming lectures on the history of philosophy. This inaugural address would become the *pre- before* the preface to the unstable and much-disputed text of the collected fragments and student transcriptions that make up Hegel's *Lectures on the History of Philosophy*. There has been a kind of bad *Aufhebung* Hegel suggests and philosophy is not doing so well. Today, both 'petty interests [*kleinen Interessen*]' and 'the deep interests of actuality [*die hohen Interessen der Wirklichkeit*]' have displaced philosophy. There is 'no place left to the higher inward life'.

Unlike Kantian reason, which always has its *own* interest (the interest of reason, *Interesse der Vernunft*), Hegel's 'spirit of the world [*Weltgeist*]' has been 'occupied [*beschäftigt*]' and distracted by these interests and has not been able to 'look within and withdraw into itself'. Now, at last, a change has come and the German nation has 'checked [*gebrochen*]' the 'stream of actuality [*Strom der Wirklichkeit*]' and 'cut its way out [*herausgehauen*] of its most material conditions'. This national *Aufhebung* has 'saved' the nationality of the German nation, which is 'the basis of all higher life' (xli; 11).

But here we are today, *28 October 1816*, Hegel says, still *hoping* that 'the Church may now resume her high position' and that philosophy may finally stop wandering in solitude (xli–xlii). This national *Aufhebung* has not entirely worked because the state itself 'has swallowed up [*verschlungen*] all other interests in its own' (xli; 11). The *interests* of the new Prussian State have 'swallowed up' *both* the petty 'interests of every-day life' and 'the deep interests of actuality' (xli–xlii). But this cannibalistic interest of the state has also become the possibility of a revival of 'the free rational world of mind' (xlii). The German nation alone in Europe has resisted the bad *Aufhebung* (Napoleon, the Napoleonic Wars); it has 'retained [*erhalten*]' philosophy while others have let it sink, 'even from memory' (xlii; 12). The bad *Aufhebung* has let philosophy go outside. At the same time, while the German nation has *retained* an externalized philosophy, a philosophy almost *hors livre*, the interest *of* the state still threatens the revival of philosophy: 'the interests of events in the world [*Interesse der großen Weltbegebenheiten*] . . . have repressed a real and earnest effort after Philosophy and driven hence any general attention to it' (xlii; 12). The German nation has both retained *and* repressed philosophy. The German nation is at once the bridge *and* the unbridgeable gap for philosophy. Today, *28 October 1816*, there is a need for an *Aufhebung* of this faulty or incomplete, this interested, *Aufhebung*. Today, we are waiting. But Hegel has begun his lectures! 'Let us together', he says, 'greet the dawn of a better time in which the spirit, hitherto a prey to externalities, may return within itself, come to itself again [*sich zurück* [*zu*] *kehren*]' (xliii; 13). Let us together bridge the unbridgeable gap.

2 November 2004.   Thinking of America today and hoping for the end of the Bush dynasty. It is the beginning of November and Hegel has started his lectures on the history of philosophy, working his way towards the Greeks, *towards* Plato. How does he get *to* Plato? How does he get to Athens, to the *agora*, to do business with Plato?

We have still not reached the preface. In the 'Inaugural Address' of 1816 Hegel looks to a time when 'true minds will rise above the interests of the moment [*Interessen des Tages*]'. At the same time, he promises his students that he will 'work with others in the interests of the higher sciences [*wissenschaftlichen Interesses*], and help to direct your way therein' (xliii; 13). An interest against an interest. The interests of the moment, of the everyday, of actuality, of events, of the state, can be counteracted only by 'the interests of the higher sciences', the interests *of* philosophy. There is a *war* of interests in the *pre-* before the preface, and Hegel opens the Prefatory Note to the *Lectures* already haunted by this war. The preface begins with the problem of the *interest* of the history of philosophy.

> In the History of Philosophy the observation is immediately forced upon us that it certainly presents great *interest* [*großes Interesse*] if its subject is regarded

from a favourable point of view, but that it would still possess *interest* [*Interesse*] even if its end were regarded as opposite to what it is. Indeed, this *interest* [*Interesse*] may seem to increase in the degree to which the ordinary conception of Philosophy, and of the end which its history serves, is reversed; for from the History of Philosophy a proof of the futility of the science is mainly derived. (my emphasis, xliv; 15)

The *history* of philosophy has its own interests and it keeps and increases this interest as it *moves* philosophy, as it inverts and reverses philosophy. For Hegel, the interest of the *history* of philosophy is unavoidable, but it must become first and foremost an interest *of* philosophy. While it is 'fair' to 'demand' that history 'should state the facts without prejudice and without any particular object or end to be gained by its means', history is 'necessarily intimately connected with the conception which is formed of it'. In the practice of history 'the relation of the events to the end regulates the selection of the facts to be recorded' (xliv). The conception, the conception of the end, at the end, regulates the history that is produced. The interest *of* philosophy should regulate the events, the *event*.

It is only this interest, this end, this 'definite conception' of 'the subject of history' that can *stop* 'history itself . . . vacillating [*Schwankendes*]' (xlv; 16). Only 'the true Notion [*Begriff*]' of philosophy as the *subject* of history can stop history wavering, tottering, swaying, swerving (xlv–vi; 16). Without a subject, history can never make a decision. For Hegel, the most important decision for a history of philosophy is the decision of the *pre-*. One should never *begin* a history of philosophy with a 'true notion' of philosophy that has *already* been 'established'. This is the first interest of philosophy *in* a history of philosophy. As we have seen, Derrida argues that the *gap* of the *pre-* in Hegelianism opens in the *need* to preface and to introduce what can *only* be 'established' as a *result*, as an end. From the start, Hegel's *Lectures on the History of Philosophy* are haunted by the end, by the premature end, by the end without a result. And always too soon, Hegel would die in the midst of his 1831 lectures on the history of philosophy.

Hegel's *Lectures* are a posthumous publication, and a much disputed, controversial and fragmented text. First published by Michelet in 1836 (and in a revised second edition in 1840–1844) and then in a new version by Hoffmeister in the 1930s and in another new version by Jaeschke and Garniron in 1993, they include fragments of Hegel's lectures and student's notes from 1805 to 1831. At least three different translations have appeared in English: Haldane and Simpson (based on Michelet's

1840–1844 text); Knox and Miller (based on Hoffmeister's text of the 1930s); and Brown and Stewart (based on the 1825–1826 lectures) (*Lectures* xviii, xxxi–xxxiv).

When it comes to Hegel's *Vorlesungen über die Geschichte der Philosophie* no one can really decide on exactly what he said, how he said it or in what order he said it. No one can really decide on what should be in and what should be out. No one is certain how Hegel would have started, or ended. With at least four different arrangements of the lectures, fragments and student notes that range over twenty-six years and one hundred and fifty-seven years from the first to the most recent edition – and the three English translations published between 1892 and 1990 – we are presented with a *history* of Hegel's *Geschichte der Philosophie*. Always too soon, death came for Hegel and we are left with the *remains*, with the *histories*, the *gaps* of a work that can never really begin or end with any certainty: the history of philosophy.

If we begin with a text, say Haldane's English translation of Michelet's second edition (Alan Bass suggests that Derrida used Hoffmeister's text, translated by Gibelin, 'The pit and the pyramid' 101), the *gaps* of the *pre-* in Hegel's *Lectures* are unavoidable. *Before* (in front of) the preface, before the conception of the end (the interest *of* philosophy), there is *already* a war of interests in the Inaugural Address from 1816. *After* (in front of) the preface, after the interest of philosophy has been stated, is the demonstration, the result, the end that the preface *needs to begin*. The Hegelian interest in the history of philosophy (on its way to Plato and beyond) is always pre-ceded by gaps. As Hegel writes in the preface and as Derrida quotes in translation in a footnote in 'Outwork':

> What can be said in this Introduction is not so much something which may be stated beforehand, as what can be justified or proved in the treatment of history. These preparatory explanations are for this reason only, not to be placed in the category of arbitrary assumptions. But to begin with stating what in their justification are really results, can only have the *interest* [*intérêt*] which may be possessed by a summary, given in advance, of the most general contents of a science. It must serve *to set aside* [*écarter* – *abzuweisen* in Hegel's text] many questions and demands which might, from our ordinary prejudices, arise in such a history. (*Lectures* xlvi; 18; 'Outwork' 18 n. 20; 27 n. 13, my emphasis)

3 November 2004. Sleepless night watching the Presidential election in America. I do not think I can bear to see Bush celebrating his victory.

We still have not reached the introduction to Hegel's *Lectures*. After the *Aufhebung of* the interest of the Inaugural Address and *as* the interest of the Prefatory Note, Hegel *begins* the Introduction to the *Lectures* with interest: 'There are various aspects under which the History of Philosophy may possess interest [*Interesse*]. We shall find the central point of this interest in the essential connection existing between what is apparently past [*Vergangenheit*] and the present [*gegenwärtigen*] stage reached by Philosophy' (1; 20). After (or before) the inaugural and prefatory interest, the introductory interest appears in the *gap* 'between what is apparently past and the present'. The interest is *in* the gap (and bridges the gap). It is through the gap (that is bridged) that 'we are what we are [*was wir sind, sind wir*]'. The 'possession of self-conscious reason', Hegel writes, 'did not grow only from the soil of the present'. *From* the gap between the past and the present *there is* thought, inheritance and tradition: a tradition that is 'alive, and swells like a mighty river which increases in size the further it advances from its source [*lebendig und schwillt als ein mächtiger Strom, der sich vergrößert, je weiter er von seinem Ursprunge aus vorgedrungen ist*]' (2–3; 21). The gap is full of water – of *Perrier* even – and through it, thanks to it, the living present swells 'the further it advances from its source'.

A deviation, a swerve (an *écart*) – 'from swerve of shore to bend of bay' (Joyce, *Finnegans Wake* 3) – from Hegel's introduction to Derrida's '*Qual Quelle*: Valéry's sources'. On *6 November 1971* Derrida delivered '*Qual Quelle*' as a conference paper at Johns Hopkins University. Marking a division *at* the beginning, he writes: 'why not ask ourselves about another outside, about the *sources set aside* [sources écartées], this time' (275; 327, trans. modified). It is from these *sources écartées*, always plural and other, that Derrida turns to Valéry's tree with ' "two *trees* within it" ', to a tree 'separated in its inside from itself [*en son dedans écarté de lui-même*] and 'cut off [*couper*] from the simple source' (276–7; 328–9, trans. modified). A singular plural. Derrida had written in 1969 of 'a singular plural, which no single origin will have ever preceded [*précédé*]' ('Dissemination' 304; 369).

4 November 2004.   Blinding November sunlight. The Hegelian aquatic logic of the gap between past and present as the opening of the history of philosophy: the further it advances – distances – itself *from* the source, the *more* the living present swells. For Derrida, in trying 'to come back to the source [*revenir à la source*]', there is *already* an overflow (*un débordement*):

The compulsive obstinacy that always leads back [*reconduit*] toward a place [*lieu*], a locus, signifies that this topos cannot become a theme or the dwelling place of a rhetoric: it rejects any presentation, any representation. It can never be there, present, *posed* before a glance, facing it; it never constitutes a present or hidden unity, an object or a subject supporting, according to the occurrence or position of the theme, a system of variations, of modulations, of transformations whose meaning or substantial content at heart would remain identical to themselves. (279; 332)

The source cannot be a theme, cannot support the theme (of the history of philosophy *as* the bridging of the gap between the past and the present): *sources écartées*. The 'de-parture [*dé-part*]' is always, in some way, a 'veering off [*virer*]' (280; 333). For Derrida, the proper meaning of the source is always secondary, always an *effect* of 'a separation and a departure [*un écart et un départ*]', of a gap and a departure (280; 333).

5 November 2004.   *Qual Quelle*. Torment (*le tourment*) Source (*la source*). Torment of the source, torment as the source through 'divisions and turns [*des écarts et des tours*]' (283; 337). Derrida takes his title, takes *Qual Quelle*, from Hegel's *Lectures on the History of Philosophy* (284–5 n. 12).

As he suggests, for Hegel gaps become *the* source when 'the source is produced only in being cut off from itself, only in taking off in its *own* negativity [*celle-ci ne se produit qu'à se couper d'elle-même, qu' à s'enlever dans sa* propre *négativité*]'. Gaps become proper, gaining propriety and property (the place). As its *'own* negativity', gaps are *put to work as* the gap *for* the source. Cut off from itself, *se couper, s'écarter*, the source is produced 'equally, *and by the same token*, in reappropriating itself, in order to amortize its own, proper death, to rebound, *se relever* [*aussi bien*, du même coup, *en se réappropriant pour amortir sa propre mort, ressauter*, se relever]' (285 n. 12; 339 n. 8). With the *same* cut, the *same* gap, *the gap that is the same*, the source amortizes the gap, reduces, fills and bridges its *own* gap. The gap bridges itself and the history of philosophy begins.

The source jumps on the gap, from the gap, raising and repeating itself. For Derrida, in raising and *repeating* itself, the *Aufhebung* of the gap can be retranslated as the *relevé* of the gap, as a raising that *already* replaces and displaces itself as it jumps on the gap, leaps from the gap. This is 'to unseal at the source the separation of an altering difference [*déceler à la source l'écart d'une différence altérante*]' (290; 345). The gap of an altering difference.

8 November 2004.   War in Fallujah. It is a month since Jacques Derrida died, sometime in the night between Friday and Saturday, a month today or tomorrow (I am still not quite sure if it was 8 or 9 October). And she said to me, sometimes it is as if you are still waiting for another letter from him.

How does one avoid monu-memorializing Jacques Derrida? How does one write about Jacques Derrida in the past tense? How does one now avoid making the work of Jacques Derrida a *monument* in the history of philosophy according to Hegel? Hegel has still not reached Plato. And we, we still have not yet reached *Glas*.

For Hegel, the history of philosophy is finished and it is time to start building monuments. 'Hegel declares the completion [*l'achèvement*] of philosophy' ('Outwork' 47; 62). In the *Lectures on the History of Philosophy*, Hegel argues that a history of philosophy must always begin with 'a general idea of the nature and the aim of the whole [*Ganze*]' (5). We must start with the whole. If we start with particulars, 'the whole is not seen for the mere details – the wood is not seen for the trees [*sieht . . . vor lauter Bäumen nicht den Wald*]' (5; 24–5).

Can there be a philosophy of trees? If a philosophy of trees were possible, a philosophy that could begin to resist the Hegelian completion of philosophy, it would perhaps have to start with the *trace*. Neither a part nor a whole and the possibility of the part–whole relation, the trace resists all induction and deduction. A philosophy of the gaps between the trees, of traces, would be an in-de-duction that can never complete itself: 'the trace as gap [*la trace comme écart*]' ('The reason of the strongest' 18).

In his 1931 preface to *Ideas I* (1913) Husserl had evoked the possibility of 'the trackless wilds of a new continent', of a land without precedent, of a land *without* tracks (15). As Ricoeur notes in the final volume of *Time and Narrative* (1985), Marc Bloch had argued in *The Historian's Craft* that the *tracks* or traces of the past are the enigmatic origin of all historiography (*Time and Narrative* III: 117, 124, 304 n. 34, 305 n. 4). [And *today* as I read this, marking *another* today, *22 May 2005*, I have just heard that Paul Ricoeur has died at the age of 92, perhaps the last of that extraordinary generation of post-war French philosophers. On Friday 20 May – the day that he died – I was in the Bodleian Library, not far from that postcard that so interested Derrida, *la carte d'Oxford*, returning to Ricoeur for the first time in many years. On Friday *8 October 2004* I had finished correcting the final proofs of my first book on Derrida, *Derrida and Disinterest*. On Sunday 10 October I heard that Derrida had died, sometime between Friday night and Saturday morning. *Depuis longtemps, si longtemps*, I had feared this day, trying to prepare, trying to avoid this day, this today, this end of the world. Before I sent off the book on Monday, I went to sit in a café in Oxford with an unread copy of *Chaque fois unique, la fin du monde* and I just had time to write in the manuscript: *Jacques Derrida (1930–2004)*. Without intending it, I had left a blank page at the beginning, a gap.]

Marc Bloch was writing *The Historian's Craft* [*Apologie pour l'histoire ou Métier d'historien*] in the midst of the Second World War (he and his wife would be shot by the Germans in 1944 for fighting with the Resistance) and his work on how one responds to the tracks and traces of the past is marked by exceptional gaps. In the introduction, he writes:

> The circumstances of my present life, the impossibility of reaching any large library, and the loss of my own books have made me dependent upon my notes and upon memory. Both the supplementary reading and the research demanded by the laws of the craft I here propose to describe have been denied me. Will it one day be granted to me to fill in the gaps? [*Me sera-t-il donné un jour de combler ces lacunes?*] (6; x)

For Bloch, all that a historian has to work with is the track or trace (*la trace*), 'the mark [*la marque*], perceptible to the senses, which a phenomena, in itself inaccessible [*en lui-même impossible à saisir*], has left behind' (55; 21, trans. modified). This mark is at once *visible*, 'perceptible to the senses,' and the remainder of a phenomena that has become *invisible*, that has become in itself (and to itself) impossible to grasp, to catch or take hold of (*en lui-même impossible à saisir*). It is because of an irreducible 'gap [*lacune*]', that this trace (is) always somewhere *between* the past and the present (61; 23).

There (are) only traces and these visible-invisible, past-present traces have fallen *outside* of consciousness, they have been 'unwittingly' left behind: they are *always* 'witnesses in spite of themselves [*les témoins malgré eux*]' (61–2; 24). They are witnesses that are never entirely *in* the archive, nor simply *outside* of the archive. They are witnesses *of* the archive that threaten the subject and the monument alike, the subject as monument: *mal d'archive*, as Derrida calls it (*Archive Fever*).

For Hegel, history – history as spirit, history on its way to the end of history as absolute knowledge – is indispensable. As Althusser noted, for Hegel 'truth is nothing without its becoming [*devenir*], [and] the becoming of truth [must] reveal itself as the truth of truth' (*Du contenu dans la pensée de G. W. F. Hegel* 61). Hegel begins his lectures with the apparent contradiction between *philosophy* (the unchangeable) and a *history* of philosophy (change). Truth does not change and a history of philosophy raises the question of the relation between *truth* and *time*:

> history tells us of that which has at one time existed, at another time has vanished, having been expelled by something else. Truth is eternal [*Wahrheit ewig ist*]; it does not fall within the sphere of the transient [*vorübergehenden*], and has no history. But if it has a history, and as this history is only the representation of a succession of past forms of knowledge, the truth is not to be found in it [*ist in ihr die Wahrheit nicht zu finden*], for the truth cannot be what has passed away [*ein Vergangenes*]. (8; 24)

As *the* truth of religion, Christianity has no history and the history of the Church must be seen as an *external* history, as the history of 'the various additions to and deviations [*Zusätze und Abirrungen*] from the truth' (9; 26). Additions to a truth that is 'found' in time – for example, geometry – can only be understood as progressive amplifications of the permanent. Such additions (supplements) can never be alterations (10). However, Hegel acknowledges, philosophy is quite different. It has neither the 'motionlessness of a complete, simple content', nor is it merely 'the onward movement of a peaceful addition' (10). The history of philosophy – truth 'found' in time – cannot entirely avoid dangerous supplements (additions that alter), nor can it exclude deviations, *écarts*.

The problem of a *history* of philosophy is also a question of literature. Philosophy is not literature. At the outset, from the *first* moment, of bridging this gap between truth and time, Hegel leaves the literary behind. The 'subjective conception' of literary works which 'produce and treat the ideas of philosophy as if they were opinions', will always be distinguished from and superseded by philosophy as 'the objective science of truth' (12). Hegel defines philosophy as 'thought . . . occupied only with itself [*Der Gedanke . . . nur mit sich selbst . . . beschäftigt*]' (5; 23). If one follows Socrates in the *Phaedo*, a history of philosophy as thought occupied *only with itself* (the soul free of the body) could only be a history of death, a history of the philosophies that begin after the death of the body.

Derrida *begins* – or ends – *The Problem of Genesis* (a text on the problem of genesis with a fifty-year history, 1953–2003) with a preface that starts with the subtitle: "History of Philosophy and Philosophy of History" (xvii). 'From the start', the twenty-three or twenty-four-year-old Derrida will write,

> we must say that we shall finish by adopting a philosophy of genesis which precisely denies the possibility of such a distinction [between the historical and the philosophical]; both through its conventions and its method, this philosophy will reveal to us [what are] the radical implications of this essential inseparability of these two worlds of meanings: history of philosophy and philosophy of history. (xvii)

From the start, for Derrida it is all about the *inseparability* of the *history* of philosophy and *philosophy* of history: an impossibility for the bridge-builders of the gap, who build bridges with traffic lights, armed checkpoints, and gaps that can be bridged and put to work. 'From the beginning of his career', the young Derrida notes, 'Husserl had formulated the demand for such a synthesis [of the historical and the philosophical]' (xix). And Derrida will close this first work with Husserl *still* seeking this synthesis. At the end of his life Husserl will write, 'I did not know that it might be so hard to die . . . Just when I am getting to the end and when everything is finished for me, I know that I must start everything again from the beginning . . .' (178).

From the start, death will surprise synthesis.

From the start, what makes Husserl's *The Origin of Geometry* (1936) so interesting for Derrida is its attempt to grapple with the historicity *of* ideal objects, with the *repetition* (the reawakening and the restitution) of the truth *as* the truth, as 'a tradition of truth' (*Introduction* 51; 'The time of a thesis' 118). In a paper given in California in 1987, 'Some statements and truisms about neologisms, newisms, postisms, parasitisms, and other small seismisms', Derrida returns to these early preoccupations. He reminds his audience that, from that start, his work has always been concerned 'with a *double gesture*' that arises from Husserl. On the one hand, Husserl argued for the possibility of a *philosophy* of history. There must be a 'critique of empirical historicism', which denies the 'original possibility of ideal objects' and is unable 'to account for something like a theorem or a philosopheme, for science, philosophy, or philosophy as science, and for any project of universal and true discourse'. On the other hand, Husserl argued for the necessity of a *history* of philosophy. Avoiding 'an ahistorical Platonism', he insisted on the description of 'the historical specificity . . . of the ideal objects of science' and 'an original or transcendental historicity' (91–2).

Husserl is always *oscillating* (one of Derrida's favoured words in *The Problem of Genesis*, and perhaps a precursor to *différance*), always swaying from side to side, always caught *between* these two incessant demands: a philosophy of history *and* a history of philosophy. Husserl is always caught in the middle and always trying, and never succeeding, to find a point of synthesis, a perfect balance. Husserl's search for the historicity *of* ideal objects, Derrida notes in his 1962 introduction to *The Origin of Geometry*, will give rise to 'an unheard-of historical intuition in which the intentional reactivation of sense should – *de jure* – precede [*précéder*] and condition the empirical determination of fact' (*Introduction* 26; 5). From the start, it is a question of precedence. Derrida will 'radicalize' Husserl's call both for the primacy of ideal objects and for the authority of transcendental historicity as original historicity ('Some statements' 92; Hobson, *Opening Lines* 20, 47–8, 56). For Derrida, an *uncertain repetition*, a repetition that re-places, a tradition that dis-places, is the only possibility for an inescapable – and impossible – historicity *of* ideal objects.

Derrida argues in 1953–1954 that Husserl had insisted that history is animated by 'the idea of philosophy', by an 'intentional rationality', that arises *in and from* Europe. At the same time, Husserl will insist that phenomenology *precedes* the rise of Europe and exceeds any historical limitation. Is the idea of philosophy then simply 'present to itself from its birth', Derrida asks? Or does it 'make itself a stranger to itself at a given moment of historical becoming'? This gap between the philosophy of history and the history of philosophy indicates that the idea of philosophy is 'not purely originary; from its birth, it negotiates with what is not it' (170). To close the gap between "truth" and "time", Husserl must rely on a Kantian *a priori* synthesis, which, like all projects of synthesis, 'must refer . . . to something other than itself'. From the start, Husserl cannot avoid 'an indefinite synthesis' in which the idea of philosophy 'loses itself in order to find in itself what it is not' and can then never entirely, completely, be identical to itself (xxiii, 170).

In *The Origin of Geometry*, Husserl gives geometry a history, or rather he gives history *to* geometry – and loses the origin.

Deleuze's *Nietzsche and Philosophy* (1962) was published in the same year as Derrida's introduction to *The Origin of Geometry*. Derrida quotes from Deleuze's book in his 1968 paper 'différance' (17) – the title without a capital, without capitalization – and has written of its influence after the death of Gilles Deleuze in 1995 ('I'm going to have to wander all alone' 192). The first few pages of Deleuze's book remain perhaps the most articulate statement of the importance of Nietzsche's concept of genealogy in Derrida's readings of Husserl on the problem of origin and genesis, philosophy and history, truth and time:

> Nietzsche attacked both the "high" idea of function which leaves values indifferent to their own origin and the idea of a simple causal derivation or smooth beginning [*d'un plat commencement*] which suggests an indifferent origin of values . . . Genealogy means both the value of origin and the origin of values . . . Genealogy signifies the differential element of values from which their value itself derives. Genealogy thus means origin or birth, but also difference or distance in the origin. (2; 2–3)

From the start, from reading Husserl on the necessity of *repetition* (of repeating – and the possibility of replacing or displacing – the origin, the truth), of *returning* (of tradition and 'the postal and epistolary reference or resonance of a communication from a distance'), and of the *risk of erasure* (of the graphic and the trace), *Derrida never stops writing about history* (*Introduction* 46–50, 94). He never stops, as he observes in his 1964 essay on Lévinas, writing about history as 'the history of the departures from totality [*l'histoire des sorties hors de la totalité*]' ('Violence and metaphysics' 117; 173). If there can be a history of the work of Jacques Derrida, it (is) *the history of the departures from totality*.

Historia, Derrida argues in *Of Grammatology* (1965–1967), has been determined as a 'detour *for the purpose of* the reappropriation of presence'. The history of philosophy has been 'the history of (the) philosophy (of presence)' (10, 14). The history of the departures from totality *begins* with the recognition that the history of philosophy as 'the history of truth, of the truth of truth' has always required the 'debasement' and 'repression' of writing (3; Royle, *After Derrida* 13–38). *Writing* history can never be reduced simply to *either* a philosophy of history *or* a history of philosophy (8, 27–8). A history of *écarts*.

'Genealogy cannot begin with the father' (*Glas* 6a).

9 November 2004.   Fighting in Fallujah. 'Discontinuity, delay, heterogeneity, and alterity already were working upon the voice, producing it from its first breath as a system of differential traces, that is as writing before the letter. Philosophical writing [according to Valéry], then, literally comes to bridge this gap, to close the dike, and to dream of virgin continuity [*colmater cette brèche, fermer la vanne et rêver la vierge continuité*]', '*Qual Quelle*' (291; 346). To bridge this gap (*colmater cette brèche*). *Brèche*: breach, opening, gap, notch, nick. *Colmater*: to seal, to plug, to fill in; (*figuré militaire*) *colmater une brèche*: to seal or close a gap, a breach in the line (*Le Robert*). The war (*polemos*) of the gap.

10 November 2004. In his introduction to *The Origin of Geometry* Derrida addresses the gap between literature and philosophy while exploring the gap between philosophy and history. Derrida contrasts Joyce to Husserl but, he argues, *both* start with Hegel. For Husserl, 'univocity removes truth out of history's reach'. Univocity is an ideality that 'remains *the same* . . . throughout all cultural developments'. It is the guarantee of 'the exactitude of translation and the purity of tradition' (101–2). It is the very possibility of 'pure history', of an 'internal history' or 'infinite historicity' (speech) that saves the truth (geometry) 'from all sensible aggression' (102, 95, 149, 152). In contrast to this claim for an absolute univocity, Derrida suggests that there are in fact *two* kinds of *equivocity*, both of which are concerned with 'a certain depth of development and concealment of a past . . . when one wishes to assume and interiorize the memory of a culture in a kind of *recollection* (*Erinnerung*) in the Hegelian sense'. Two Hegelian equivocities: one which works towards Hegel and one which wanders away and exceeds the Hegelian totality. There is Husserl (who attempts to reduce the empirical to the univocal) and Joyce (who attempts to 'explore' history '*within* the *labyrinthian* field of culture' by making 'the structural unity of all empirical culture appear in the generalized equivocation of a writing') (102, 103–4). Two equivocities: the *gaps* between philosophy and literature, and between the philosophy of history and the history of philosophy. Derrida is already sketching out the relation between philosophy and literature and the history of philosophy that will dominate much of his later work.

Having excluded the literary (as a 'subjective construction') in the *Lectures on the History of Philosophy* from the first moment of the first step in the resolution of the contradiction between a history of philosophy and a philosophy of history, Hegel encapsulates or summarizes the relationship between literature and philosophy as the long-standing opposition between opinion (*Meinung*) and science (*Wissenschaft*), *doxa* and *epistēmē* (14; 32). If one accepts the authority of *doxa* there is no truth (in history), there is only a diversity of disconnected particulars that cancel each other out: 'these individual points of view are thus foreign [*fremdes*] to me: my thinking reason is not free, nor is it present in them: for me they are but extraneous, dead historic matter [*toter, historischer Stoff*]' (15; 33). The sovereignty of *doxa* (of literature) turns the *history* of philosophy into military history and a study of the dead superseding the dead: 'the whole [*Ganze*] of the history of Philosophy becomes a battlefield covered with the bones of the dead; it is a kingdom [*ein Reich*] not merely formed of dead and lifeless individuals [*vergangener . . . leiblich verstorbener Individuen*], but of refuted and spiritually dead systems [*geistig vergangener Systeme*], since each has killed and buried the other' (17; 35). There can *only* be a history of philosophy, a *living* history, when we come to recognize the whole in the part and the part in the whole, 'the particular form in which a universality finds its actuality' (18).

'If the formula for this absolute knowledge can be thought about and put in question,' Derrida will write in 1972 in 'Outwork', 'the whole is treated then by a "part"["*partie*"] bigger than itself; this is the strange subtraction of a *remark* whose theory is borne by dissemination and which constitutes the whole, necessarily, as a *totality-effect*' (54; 71). ' "Literature" . . . transforms the whole into a part [*transforme le tout en partie*]' (56; 73). "Literature" is 'a part [*pièce*], that, within *and* without the whole, marks the wholly other, the other incommensurate with the whole' (56; 74). For Derrida, if there is history, it is a history of departures from totality that cannot exclude literature: *the traces of parts exceeding wholes.*

If there is history, for Derrida it is a history *neither* of the dead (of dead particulars) *nor* of the living (of living universals inhabiting and connecting particulars), but – if such a narrative is possible – of *life death* (*la vie la mort*), of that which exceeds the absolute inversions of either life *as* death (Nietzsche, Freud) or death *as* life (Plato, Hegel) (*Derrida and Disinterest* 109–25). *la vie la mort* (without any capital or capitalization): 'a structure of alteration without opposition' ('To speculate' 285), marking 'the gap of an altering difference [*l'écart d'une différence altérante*]' ('*Qual Quelle*' 290; 345).

Écarts: deviations, digressions, swerves, separations, alterations. For Hegel, *the* gap is always put to work in the history of philosophy, but there are no *gaps* in the history of philosophy. In the introduction to the *Lectures,* Hegel speculates on the gap to move beyond the opposition of *doxa* and *epistēmē*. As we have seen, for Derrida, 'what can look at itself is not one: and . . . one plus one makes at least three' (*Of Grammatology* 36). As it marks itself, dialectical speculation loses itself in the 'the excess of a re-mark' ('Outwork' 21). One becomes at least three and three becomes at least four. For Hegel, the 'highest end' is the 'coming-to-self of Mind' in which thought becomes *objective* by becoming its *own* object (*Lectures* 23, 21). As Derrida observes in 'The pit and the pyramid' (1968), objectivity and interiority 'are only apparently opposed, since idealization has as its meaning (from Plato to Husserl) the simultaneous confirmation of objectivity and interiority one by the other. Ideal objectivity maintains its identity with itself, its integrity and its resistance all the more in no longer depending upon an empirical sensuous exteriority' (93 n. 21). For both Descartes and Spinoza, the objectivity *of* the mind was made possible by the *idea* of God. For Hegel, desiring above all to become its own object, thought speculates on itself to find itself, divides and doubles itself – creates its other – *without* being altered and 'manifests what is contained in it so that it may return to itself': one becomes an *ersatz* two (22). 'The development of Mind', Hegel concludes, 'lies in the fact that its . . . separation constitutes its coming to itself' (23). Thought makes its *own* gap, makes the gap its *own*: a gap that recollects itself. For a history *of* truth to be possible, thought must always open *and* close the gap.

'It is always necessary to ask oneself why and on top of what one presses to leap [*Il faut toujours se demander pourquoi et par-dessus quoi l'on se presse de sauter*]' (*Glas* 216; 242).

As Derrida notes in 'Outwork', Heidegger invokes the leap (*ressaut*) in *Identity and Difference* (31 n. 30; 43 n. 17). For Heidegger, the leap (*Sprung*) springs *away* from metaphysics (from 'man as rational animal', from 'being interpreted as ground', from technology as a totality of planning, calculation and manipulation) and leaps *towards* an authentic belonging (the 'mutual appropriation' of man and Being) (32–5; 96–9). This springing away and leaping towards opens an abrupt 'unbridged' *gap* (33). This gap displaces the primacy of man founded on a limited and limiting understanding of technology. The spring, the leap (and the gap that it opens) *facilitates* a framework (*Ge-Stell*) – a view or structure (a *tekhnē*) beyond what is present, beyond presence – as the possibility of 'the event of appropriation' (*Ereignis*) of man and Being (36; 100). The event (an untranslatable singularity) then overcomes and transforms the frame and language, the delicate vibration of the event, serves thinking (37–8). For Heidegger, the spring (and the gap that it opens) indicates 'a time of thinking which is different from the time of calculation' (41). Heidegger's gap is always a gap *of* thinking (*Of Grammatology* 93). And like the gap of Hegel, it is a gap that opens *and* closes. The leap (and the gap) *opens* (resisting the primacy of man, the totality of calculation), but it also *closes* (bringing man and Being *together* in an architecture of the event that uses and then *supersedes* the frame).

Derrida *stops* at the frame, and *twists* its edges.

11 November 2004. Armistice day. Yasser Arafat has died in Paris. There is, as far as I know, only one work by Derrida with *écart* in the title, though the first book *on* Derrida, published in 1973, was entitled *Écarts: Quatre essais à propos de Jacques Derrida* (with essays by Finas, Kofman, Laporte and Rey) and Catherine Malabou entitled her reading of Derrida in *Counterpath* (1999), 'L'écartement des voies' ('The parting of the ways'). In 1970, between the texts that make up *Dissemination* and *Margins of Philosophy*, those extended footnotes to the two columns of *Glas*, Derrida published a short article in *Les temps modernes* on an *écart*, an *écart* of the other, an *écart* that was not his own, an *écart* in a state of war.

How would one translate the title: 'D'un texte à l'écart'? Of a text on the side? Of a text put aside? Of a wandering text? Text off track? From a text to the gap? Derrida's title is a response to an article by Jacques Garelli, 'L'écart du maintenant et l'extension de l'esprit' (1969), attacking Derrida's 1968 essay '*Ousia* and *Grammē*: Note on a Note in *Being and Time*'. Derrida responds to this polemical *écart* with a sidestep, *à l'écart*. In other words, he responds to *l'écart du maintenant* – to the *écart of* the now – with an *écart* that wanders, deviates and swerves (*l'écart à l'écart*).

In this war of *écarts*, Derrida notes that Garelli charges that in '*Ousia* and *Grammē*', Hegel and Heidegger 'are never quoted and that is why their texts are put aside [*mis à l'écart*] at the very moment when they are aimed at by my *Note*' (1547). Derrida argues that while he is attacked for putting aside, putting in the background, sidelining the texts of Hegel and Heidegger, Garelli himself 'keeps back [*tient à l'écart*] . . . a certain number of texts' (1547). Derrida goes on to cite the passages in '*Ousia* and *Grammē*' 'that M. Garelli rules out [*écarte*] for the sake of expediency' (1548). 'In short,' Derrida writes, 'he dismisses my text [*il écart mon texte*]' (1548). Derrida concludes by demonstrating how Garelli 'maintains . . . his "écart" [*maintenant . . . son "écart"*] (1549, 1552). For Derrida, in this war of *écarts*, the *écart* in Garelli's title, '*l'écart du maintenant*', reinforces not only his departure from Derrida's text, but also his maintenance of the gap *of* the now, of the gap as the presence of the present.

There can always be a war of gaps. *Écarts* are always a risk. Gaps always risk being dismissed, pushed aside, or put to work (*Le toucher* 322). Gaps also risk being celebrated and idealized as an *absolute* transgression, as if there could be 'a theory of transgressive gaps [*écarts*]' that presumes to do without *both* the constraints of convention *and* the unforeseeable 'inventions of the other' ('Psyche: Inventions of the other' 41 [33], 43–4). But one can never simply make one's own gap, make the gap one's own. There are always gaps. There is war. It is – it was – 10:46, fourteen minutes before the eleventh hour of the eleventh month of 2004.

Gaps always risk being put to work, and a history of gaps most of all. As Derrida says in an interview from 1971, a year after his war of gaps:

> But in asking about the historicity of history, about what permits us to call "histories" these histories irreducible to the reality of a general history, the issue is precisely not to return to a question of the Socratic type. The issue is rather to show that the risk of metaphysical reappropriation is ineluctable, that it happens very fast, as soon as the question of the concept and of meaning, or of the essentiality that necessarily regulates the risk, is asked. (*Positions* 58)

The Socratic question will always be a question of 'a definition of essence', of the search for a general concept of history founded on the reconstitution of 'a system of essential predicates'. The Socratic question will always return history to ontology (*Positions* 58–9).

For Hegel, the question of the history of philosophy begins (or has already ended) with the opposition between opinion (*doxa*) and science (*epistēmē*). Hegel is starting where Plato already started. For Plato, Derrida notes in 'Plato's pharmacy' (1968), the second work in *Dissemination*, writing is 'productive not of science but of opinion' (103; 128, trans. modified). Those who write are 'fake or self-proclaimed wise men (*doxosophoi*)', Sophists (105–6; *Phaedrus* 275b). As Derrida observes in 'White mythology' (1971), the Sophists always raise the question of a gap *for* Plato, of the gap *in* Plato, of 'an ideal that is produced in the separation [*dans l'écart*] (and order) between philosophy or dialectics on the hand and (sophistic) rhetoric on the other' (224; 267). Plato needs the Sophists and he is always trying to get away from them. He needs the gap and he is always trying to close it. Without Plato defeating the Sophists one cannot even begin a history of philosophy. The Sophist believes that virtue can be taught. He uses the art (*tekhnē*) of persuasion to sell and make a profit from the knowledge of virtue. He is a trader, a speculator, 'a paid hunter', in virtue (*Sophist* 222–4).

How does the tenured professor, for example Professor Hegel, sidestep (*écarte*) the fact that he is being paid to teach virtue? 'Perhaps', as Derrida remarks at the beginning of *Glas*, 'here is an incompatibility (rather than a dialectical contradiction) between the teaching and the signature' (*Glas* 1a). 'I have dedicated my life to Science', Hegel insists on *28 October 1816*,

> and it is a true joy to me to find myself again in this place where I may, in a higher measure and more extensive circle, work with others in the interests of the higher sciences, and help to direct your way therein. I hope that I may succeed in deserving and obtaining your confidence. But in the first place, I ask nothing of you but to bring with you, above all, a trust in science and a trust in yourselves. (xliii)

It is a very persuasive performance. I've done this most of my life and here I am doing it again, and with others, so you can trust me. But 'in the first place', which, rhetorically is already the second place, 'trust in science' and 'trust in yourselves'. After me, after science (which I've know a long time and am here 'to direct your way therein', so it is really trusting me again), trust in yourself. Much like Socrates in the *Phaedo* waiting finally to do philosophy after he has died, it is all a matter of trust.

One could digress here on Derrida's 1977 essay 'The age of Hegel', but I don't have a copy at hand *today* and this is the constraint and the finitude of *writing with the date*, of writing *from* the date, from *12 October 2004*. Everything, except what is written today, in *one* day (the diary entry, the poem, the short story, the newspaper article), everything that is written, excludes all its *todays*, all its *décalages* (gaps, time differences). Perhaps most noticeably in 'Envois' (1980), but also in 'Cartouches' (1978), 'LIVING ON. Border Lines' (1979), 'Circumfession' (1991), *Veils* (1998) and *Counterpath* (1999), Derrida has written *with* the date, with the gaps of the date.

'Insist on the *écart*', he writes on *6 December 1977* ('Cartouches' 192).

Derrida first explicitly dates his text in 'The ends of man', a paper given in New York in October 1968:

> and then to the writing of this text, which I date [*je date*] quite precisely from the month of April 1968: it will be recalled that these were the weeks of the opening of the Vietnam peace talks and of the assassination of Martin Luther King. A bit later, when I was typing this text, the universities were invaded by the forces of order – and for the first time at the demand of a rector – and then reoccupied by the students in the upheaval you are familiar with. This

historical and political horizon would call for a long analysis. I have simply found it necessary to mark, date [*les marquer, les dater*], and make known to you the historical circumstances [*les circonstances historiques*] in which I prepared this communication. These circumstances appear to me to belong, by all rights [*de plein droit*], to the field and the problematic of our colloquium. (114; 135)

From at least 'The ends of man', Derrida has dated, in one way or another, almost all of his texts. Derrida is always writing about history, about the political and the question of the institution (Bennington and Young, *The Question of History* 1–11).

The *work*, the work of philosophy, of history, of literature, of writing, is almost always presented as a seamless continuity: a work of months, years, not days; wholes, not parts; parts, not traces. The part is never bigger than the whole and as Kant had said, '*in mundo non datur hiatus, non datur saltus* [in the world there is no hiatus, there is no leap]' (*Critique of Pure Reason* A 229/B 282). The work without its *todays* erases all the time, all the gaps, all the leaps, all the finitude, all the mortality, all the mourning, all the precariousness of its unforeseeable, inadmissible *todays*.

As Herodotus, that great Presocratic philosopher, has Solon say to Croesus: 'Of all those days not one brings to him anything exactly the same as another. So Croesus, man is entirely what befalls him' (*The History*, trans. Grene 47 [I. 32]).

10 December 1977

Must do the impossible. Get back down to it today. To work, of course.
Of mourning. Make mourning *one's* mourning [do one's mourning of mourning]. That's what I call doing the impossible. ('Cartouches' 211)

12 November 2004. *Today*, a deviation, a swerve, a digression: an *écart*. It is almost the first word of *Being and Time*: *heute*, today. Heidegger writes: 'This question [the question of Being] has today [*heute*] been forgotten, even though in our time [*unsere Zeit*] we deem it progressive to give our approval to "metaphysics" again' (H2, trans. modified). The question of being has been forgotten (*Vergessenheit*) *today*. But what is the today of *Being and Time*? Heidegger dedicates *Being and Time* to Husserl on '8 April 1926' and writes in the 1953 preface that the book was published 'in the Spring of 1927'. The *today* of *Being and Time* is the today of 1926 *or* 1927: the today *of* 1926–1927. It is a today that *slides* across two dates, two years. It is an indeterminate, mobile today; a today that already is *at once* of this very day (8 April 1926, Husserl's sixty-seventh birthday) *and* of another day (a day in the Spring of 1927). As Derrida suggests in *Schibboleth – pour Paul Celan* (1984–1986), when I write *today* it can indicate this very day *and* any and everyday – there is always today *and* another day, the other of today (*Derrida and Disinterest* 103–7).

At the opening of his 1996 paper on Artaud, *Artaud le Moma: Interjections d'appel* (1996–2002), Derrida writes:

'And who/today/will say/what?' ['*Et qui/aujourd'hui/dira/quoi*'] . . . These words, I repeat them, they precede us [*précèdent*] and not only in time. They are before us and in front of us [*Ils sont avant nous et devant nous*]. Today, when is this? [*Aujourd'hui, c'est-à-dire quand*?] Today, at this moment, someone is going to sign, asking themselves 'and who/today/will say/what,' today, 16 October 1996, it is 2 July 1947. (13–14)

Today we have forgotten the question of being. Could one still forget the question of being *without* the today that launches *Being and Time*? Is this today indispensable for the repetition-restating-retrieval of the question of being (*Wiederholung der Seinsfrage*)? This *first* today in the opening of the introduction is not the first – or the last – today of *Being and Time*. In the preface (the first *and* the last word) (1927), Heidegger asks: 'Do we in our time have an answer to the question of what we really mean by the word 'being'?' (H1). Macquarrie and Robinson have translated this as 'our time', but Heidegger uses *heute* here: do we *today* have an answer to what we really mean by the word 'being'? Heidegger then follows this *question* (of the preface) with an opening statement (of the introduction): *today* we have *forgotten* the question of being. At the outset, today, we can *only* ask if we have an answer to a question that we can *only* forget.

Before – and after – the 1927 preface there is the 1953 preface to the seventh edition of *Being and Time*. This preface appears as the first – and the last – word on *Being and Time*. Looking back to the first printing of *Being and Time* in 1927, Heidegger justifies the 'unchanged' 'First Half' of his uncompleted project. He writes: 'Yet the road it has taken remains even today [*bleibt indessen auch heute noch*] a necessary one, if our Dasein is to be stirred by the question of Being' (H17). The path (*Weg*) of *Being and Time* remains (*bleibt*), 'yet . . . even today' (*indessen . . . heute noch*) 'a necessary one'. Even today, still today (*heute noch*), after twenty-six years, the path taken by *Being and Time* is necessary.

How is one to understand this first and last today? How is one to distinguish this today of 1953 from the today of 1926–1927? *Heute noch, still* today the today of 1926–1927 is relevant: *nothing* has changed, the today of 1953 makes no difference. *Heute noch*, *even* today in 1953, when so much has happened, when *everything* has changed, the today of 1926–1927 that launched *Being and Time*, that made *Being and Time* possible, 'remains . . . necessary'. *Heute noch*: nothing has changed *or* everything has changed. It is a question of nothing *or* everything. And can a today *remain*? Is the today of 1926–1927 the *same* today as the today of 1953? Does the today of *Being and Time* have any time, any history? Is it always today? Is there any yesterday, any tomorrow, not only *in* the work *Being and Time*, but also *for* the work *Being and Time*?

The question of being, Heidegger writes in the introduction, has been forgotten *today* because 'Greek ontology and its history . . . determine the conceptual character of philosophy even today [*noch-heute*]' (H21). This today (the today *of* 1926–1927–1953) is even today a Greek today, a today *of* yesterday. For Heidegger, it is precisely because this today is a today *of* yesterday that his critical destruction of ontology does not relate itself towards the past: 'its criticism is aimed at 'today' [*ihre Kritik trifft das* "*Heute*"] and at the prevalent way of treating the history of ontology' (H22). *Being and Time* is aimed at "*Heute*".

How does one *aim* at "*Heute*"? This is really an *impossible* question of quotation marks. Why does Heidegger sometimes refer to today in *Being and Time* without quotation marks and sometimes with quotation marks? There is no apparent consistency in Heidegger's use of quotation marks (see for example H391). What are the strange graphics of today in *Being and Time*? From this first appearance of "today" in the introduction one could say that the quotation marks are a kind of shorthand for the today that is *of* yesterday, for the pervasive influence of ontology *today*. At the same time, Derrida suggests in *Of Spirit* (1987) that quotation marks in Heidegger's work describe a particular critical strategy. Heidegger places the word *spirit* (*Geist*) in quotation marks, using it 'in its deconstructed sense to designate something other which resembles it, of which it is, as it were, the metaphysical ghost, the spirit of another spirit. Between the quotation marks, through the grid they impose, one sees a double of spirit announcing itself' (24; 37). For Derrida, a "today" in quotation marks would 'never be present to itself' ('Pas' 28). Is Heidegger's "*Heute*" the same old day (an Athenian day) or is it the double, the ghost of today, 'something other which resembles it', a today that is always more and less than *today*?

For Heidegger, 'average *everydayness* [*Alltäglichkeit*]' is the best 'way of access' to *Dasein* (H16–17). Everydayness is 'that way of existing in which Dasein maintains itself 'every day' ["*alle Tage*"]' (H370). It is a way of existing 'by which Dasein is dominated through and through' by 'the comfortableness of the accustomed' (H370–1). With 'everydayness', Heidegger argues, 'everything is all one and the same', and 'that which will come tomorrow [*das Morgige*] . . . is 'eternally yesterday's' ["*ewig Gestrige*"]'. With everydayness there is *nothing new*. It is always today: 'like yesterday, so today and tomorrow ["*wie gestern, so heute und morgen*"]'. At the same time, this nothing new is strange, uncanny; everydayness is an 'enigma', a 'bewildering phenomenon' in which 'in living unto its days Dasein *stretches* itself *along* 'temporally' in the sequence of those days' (H371). The *nothing new* announces the enigma of temporality.

'The sun shone, having no alternative, on the nothing new. Murphy sat out of it, as though he were free, in a mew in West Brompton' (Samuel Beckett, *Murphy* 5).

The everyday is also the source of a necessary inauthentic involvement, a distracting preoccupation with today. 'Everyday Dasein [*Das alltägliche Dasein*]', Heidegger writes, 'has been dispersed [*zerstreut*] into many kinds of things which daily [*täglich*] "come to pass" ' (H389). Caught up in the everydayness of the daily, *Dasein* endures '*dispersion* and *disconnectedness* [Zerstreuung *und dem* Unzusammenhang]' (H390). The inauthentic today scatters and separates the 'there'. It is the resolute reaction *against* this 'distraction' of today that gives *Dasein* 'constancy' and is the *origin* of 'the self' maintaining itself 'through a certain self-sameness' (H390, H373). Without today, there could be no self.

Heidegger goes on to link this distracting sameness of the everyday to the inauthenticity of *curiosity*. Curiosity is a mode of the inauthentic "*making present*" (gegenwärtigen), of a present without the future (H338). It is a 'craving for the new [*dem Neuen*]' (H347). It 'seeks novelty [*Neue*] only in order to leap from it anew to another novelty [*Neuem*]' (H172). Leaping from the new to the new, it is a "*making present*" that always runs *away* from the future possibilities that would bring itself back to itself as an authentic 'moment of vision'. It is a running away from 'the awaiting of a definite possibility' (H347). Curiosity is the *everything new*: the mirror image of the nothing new.

The historicality of Dasein as a '*handing down* to oneself [*Sichüberliefern*]' of the 'authentic possibilities of existence' provides a way of *counteracting* 'the 'average' public way of interpreting *Dasein* today [*heutigen*]' (H383). Historicality gives *Dasein* a resource to reclaim the *future* possibilities of its *own past* (for Lévinas, in contrast, the past is always the trace *of* the other) and to claim a today *of* tomorrow. Today must be taken away from the perspective of the 'they' which only sees today as the nothing new and the everything new. In 'inauthentic historicality . . . the way in which fate has been primordially stretched along has been hidden. With the inconstancy of the they-self Dasein makes present its 'today' ["*Heute*"]. In awaiting the next new thing, it has already forgotten the old one' (H391). Since it is 'lost in the making present of the today [*Heute*]', the 'they' always 'understands the 'past' in terms of the 'Present' '. For Heidegger, it is only 'the temporality of authentic historicality, as the moment of vision of anticipatory repetition, [that] *deprives* the "today" of its character as present [*Entgegenwärtigung des Heute*], and weans one from the conventionalities of the "they" ' (H391). Today (*Heute* or "*Heute*") must be historicized, temporalized and deprived of the present (H397). Deprived of the present, *today* is open to the future and no longer blind to its own *finitude*.

For Heidegger, there is a today *of* yesterday (a Greek today), there is a today *of* today (the everyday, the nothing new *or* the everything new) and there is the today *of* tomorrow (the today deprived of the present, the other of today): the todays of Heidegger. Having said all of this, it also seems that the today of Heidegger's 1953 preface is an eminently Greek and very average today, an either/or today, and a today that is *tormented* by an impossible decision (a decision *from* the impossible). Heidegger's today in *Being and Time* is the today of 1926–1953: it is a today that can *neither* accept that nothing has changed (since 1926) *nor* that everything has changed (since 1926). Even today (*heute noch*), today still remains an open question in the prefaces to *Being and Time*. It is a question of the pre-cedence of today (of the other of today, of the today that is at once before us *and* in front of us) that Heidegger could still not answer in 1953.

14 November 2004.   'Here we are, Socrates, true to our agreement of yesterday' (216). The *Sophist* begins as an ending to the *Theaetetus*, as the tomorrow of yesterday, as the preface that is, already, a post-face: a very Hegelian beginning. How does one, right from the start, avoid the Sophist? The Stranger from Elea begins his dialectic against the Sophists by making a distinction between the art of producing (bringing into existence what did not exist before) and the art of acquisition (working from and with what has already been produced) (219). From the start, it is clear that the Stranger is no Socrates (who silently listens). He makes Plato's customary unreliable narrator (Socrates), appear as the epitome of reliability. The Stranger associates learning (knowledge, wisdom and virtue) with acquisition. In other words, learning is not innate; it is acquired through education, custom and convention. This is the argument of Protagoras, the Sophist who writes (*Protagoras* 323, *Sophist* 232). But at the same time, he argues that *mimēsis* is part of the art of producing (219, 265). From the start, there is a dubious choice (dubious for Socrates) between convention and *mimēsis*. As Derrida observes in 'Entre deux coups de dés' ('Between two throws of dice'), an unpublished text with only a title and a few fragmentary passages collected in the footnotes of 'The double session', 'It is impossible to pin *mimēsis* down [*immobilser*] to a binary classification or, more precisely, to assign a single place to the *tekhnē mimētikē* within the "division" set forth in the *Sophist*' (186 n. 14; 229 n. 8). The Stranger goes on to link the Sophist with the art of acquisition and its sub-groups of the secret forceful conquest or hunting of men (for money) through the art of persuasion (219, 222). Sophists are hunters. But at the same time, in this 'mimodrama' as Derrida calls it, as the Stranger and Theaetetus attempt to pursue and to define the 'many sided animal' that is the Sophist, they become hunters (226a) ('The double session' 186 n. 14). And reason, the Stranger says, 'is lord of the hunt' (235c).

The Stranger gives all the actions that imply a 'notion of division' the 'one name' of 'the art of discriminating [*diakritikēn*]' and defines this 'one name' as a kind of 'separation' (226b–d, trans. modified). As Hegel would learn from Plato, this is a separation (an *écart*) always on the path to purification. If it begins with separation, 'the art of dialectic' should always 'arrive at purification' through the refutation of supposed knowledge (227a, 230d–e; *Signsponge* 75). The gaps do not wander or swerve (*l'écart à l'écart*). While this should clearly discriminate (*écarter*) the philosopher from the Sophist, Theaetetus remarks, 'yet the Sophist has a certain likeness to our minister of purification'. 'Yes,' the Stranger responds, 'the same sort of likeness which a wolf, who is the fiercest of animals, has to a dog, who is the gentlest.' Sophists are like wolves and philosophers are like dogs. The Stranger quickly warns against such comparisons, 'for they are most slippery things' (231a). The Stranger, the man without a name, goes on (once again) to separate the philosopher from the Sophist by arguing that the Sophist has a 'multiplicity of names'. As he has 'one name and many kinds of knowledge, there must be something wrong' (232a).

This early denial of interdisciplinary studies, leads the Stranger to his key point: the Sophists claim to understand *all* things, to be able to dispute about *all* things. Claiming to know and to be able to do *everything*, they have a 'conjectural or apparent knowledge . . . which is not the truth' (233c). Sophists claim 'absolute power' and this claim makes them imitators, magicians and mimics. The Sophist claims *absolute* knowledge and this can only be 'the imitative art' akin to that of the painter who makes 'all things' by making 'resemblances of real things which have the same name with them' (234–5). The claim to the absolute can only be an act of imitation. Hegel, as Derrida points out, would both agree and disagree with this. He would agree, because any (naïve) claim to an absolute only *invites* the *Aufhebung* and history as spirit: 'Hegel thought absolute difference, and showed that it can be pure only by being impure' ('Violence and metaphysics' 320 n. 91). He would disagree, because Plato (who cannot entirely avoid being a Sophist and 'imitates the imitators in order to restore the truth of what they imitate: the truth itself', 'Plato's pharmacy' 108, 112) already suggests that any claim to the absolute, to absolute knowledge as the end of the history as spirit *can* be, and *might* be, only an imitation, a mime of the truth, a mime *without* the truth.

And why is Socrates so quiet? Why does the man who never stops asking questions, say nothing? If Socrates starts speaking perhaps he will become, will no longer be able to be distinguished from, the Sophist. The Sophist is the gap for Plato. He launches philosophy, makes Socrates possible *and* he opens a mourning for philosophy (for the proper name, the proper name of philosophy), right from the start. Can Hegel still *begin* the history of philosophy when there is a question of Socrates the Sophist?

15 November 2004. The Sophist imitates absolute knowledge and 'runs away into the darkness of non-being' (254a). It is only the hunter of the Sophist who appreciates that non-being is 'unthinkable, unutterable, unspeakable, indescribable': nothing (238c). On the other side of nothing, the Stranger and Theaetetus start hunting for being and come, 'unawares', to philosophy.

Being cannot *always* be in motion, nor can it *always* be in rest. It must be *both* movable and immovable. Motion and rest cannot *be* absolute. Nor, if there is motion *and* rest, can they *be* the same: one cannot have motion *as* rest or rest *as* motion. In other words, being is *at once* motion and rest *and* neither motion nor rest. Not absolute, not the same, being (in relation to

43

motion and rest) must be different. Being must be 'some third thing', 'something different' (249–50). But if being does not 'participate' in motion and rest, there can *be* no motion or rest. However, if it does participate, not only is there no 'universal motion' or 'universal rest', but being itself would not be 'immutable and everlasting', absolute (252).

What would Derrida say about this hunt for being? Apparently neither absolute nor simply the same nor merely different, the relation of being to motion and rest threatens the clear distinction between being and non-being, the 'unthinkable, unutterable, unspeakable, indescribable'. For being to be in motion or to be at rest, it is already exposed – it exposes the "is" – to the risk of the too fast *and* the too slow, to the *speeds*, the traces of *différance* (*Derrida and Disinterest* 92–108). Neither absolute, nor the same, the relation of being to motion and rest marks *différance* as the possibility *and* the limitation of ontology. The relation of being to motion and rest: differing *and* deferring being *as* being – without rest. As Derrida observes, even the Stranger cannot avoid admitting that in 'differing from Being, the other is always relative' ('Violence and metaphysics' 127).

For Plato, and for that great reader of Plato, Hegel, philosophy separates itself from sophistry when the philosopher recognizes that in 'dialectical science' division, separation, 'neither makes the same other, nor makes the other same'. There is philosophy (the science of the truth) when the philosopher can see *clearly* the one *in* the many and the many *in* the one (253). Being is at once motion and rest, neither simply motion nor rest *and*, at the same time, is *absolute*. The Stranger from Elea insists that 'being [*ón*], and difference or other [*eteron*], traverse all things and mutually interpenetrate, so that the other partakes of being, and by reason of this participation is, and yet is not of that which it partakes, but other, and being other [*eteron*] than being [*òntos*], it is clearly a necessity that not-being should be [*eiai mē ón*]' (259a). In relation to motion and rest, being is different (at once being *and* not being, which is *always* a difference *of* being) *and* absolute (256–8). Whatever the other does, the other *is*. For Hegel, this will be the possibility of the history of philosophy because it already announces the end of history.

'When I introduced the word 'is', did I not contradict what I said before?' (238e).

'And the philosopher, always holding converse through reason with the idea of being, is also dark from excess of light' (254a).

'We are', Derrida writes in 'Plato's pharmacy', 'today on the eve of Platonism [*aujourd'hui à la veille du platonisme*]. Which can also, naturally, be thought of as the morning after [*lendemain*] Hegelianism.' The Sophist and the writer both *mime* the truth and 'according to a relation that philosophy would call simulacrum', the *epistēmē* is 'assumed and at the same time displaced into a completely different field, where one can still, but that's all, "mime absolute knowledge" '. A 'different field', that puts not only Plato but also the Sophist as the other *of* Plato in question (107–8; 133–4). The supplement, writing as the supplement to memory (the copy, the duplicate) is dangerous for both Plato and *his* Sophist, *his* other, because it is neither being (*ón*) nor not-being (*mē ón*). The supplement – the 'trace through which the present increases itself in the act of disappearing' – is a sliding (*glissement*) that slips away (*dérobe*) from this 'simple alternative' that sustains Plato's clear separation of *doxa* and *epistēmē*, Sophist and philosopher, and makes Hegel's history of philosophy possible (109–10; 136–7).

And in 'Plato's pharmacy', Derrida notes, Gorgias *writes*: 'speech . . . can stop fear and banish grief [*écarter le deuil*]' (116; 144).

16 November 2004. Colin Powell resigned yesterday (we in the provinces of the empire hear that the consul has resigned, but the emperor is mad and has appointed a horse as his new consul). For Plato, where there is a gap, there is a bridge:

> Plato imitates the imitators in order to restore the truth of what they imitate: truth itself. Indeed only truth as the presence (*ousia*) of the present (*on*) is here discriminative. And its powers to discriminate [*son pouvoir discriminant*], which commands or, as you will, is commanded by the difference between the signified and the signifier, in any case remains systematically inseparable from that difference. Now this discrimination itself becomes so subtle that eventually it separates nothing, in the final analysis, but the same from itself [*ne séparer jamais . . . que le même de soi*], from its perfect, almost indistinguishable double. This is a movement that produces itself entirely within the structure of ambiguity and reversibility of the *pharmakon*. ('Plato's pharmacy' 112; 139 trans. modified)

Derrida turns to the question of Hegel and the bridge in 'The pit and the pyramid' (1968). 'In determining being as presence', he writes, 'metaphysics could treat the sign only as a *transition* [*un* passage, *Übergehen*] . . . As the site of transition [*lieu de passage*], the bridge [*passerelle*] between two moments of full presence, the sign can function only as a *provisional* reference [*renvoi*] of one presence to another. The bridge can be *lifted*

[*La passerelle peut être* relevée]' (71; 82). 'The pit and the pyramid' is an essay about the bridge, but not simply as the bridge (*le pont*), but as the footbridge or gangway (*la passerelle*), as the temporary walkway or narrow passageway, as the gangplank used to board an opening in the side of a ship. As Derrida tells us in *Counterpath* (1999), it is from these gangways that he *began travelling*, taking his 'first departure' in 1949 on a boat from Algeria to Marseilles and his first voyage in 1956–1957 to and back from America on the same ship, *Le Liberté* (290–1). One can see a photograph of Derrida on the *Liberté* in 1957, *after* he has used the gangway to leave New York and *before* he has used it to arrive in France: travelling – between gangplanks (25).

The gangway is always a risk. Between the dock and the ship, it crosses the narrow space, the temporary chasm of the water, the sea, the ocean below. For Hegel, as Derrida notes at the outset, the sign (and language) as the 'middle term' in the spiritual world is 'the analogue' of *water* as the middle term in the material world (71). The sign is the bridge, the gangway, *over* the water and, analogously, it *is* the water. The middle term, the '*provisional* reference [*renvoi*]', is both the bridge *and* the gap, the bridge *as* the gap. Both bridge and gap, it is *also* the possibility of the irreducible gap, of the gap that *cannot* be bridged, of the gap that swerves and wanders (*l'écart à l'écart*), like waves in the sea.

The gangway can be *lifted* (*la passerelle peut être* relevée). The gangway can be lifted and the voyage begins: the Hegelian *Aufheben* and Derridian *relever*. And gaps are already at work: 'In order to mark *effectively* the displacements of the sites of conceptual inscription, one must articulate the systematic chains of the movement according to their proper generality and their proper period, according to their unevenesses [*leur décalages*, their jutting out and standing back, their shifting forward and shifting back]' (72; 83). Within these 'systematic chains' are the links between the sign and the imagination. The *Aufhebung* and the *Erinnerung* of sensible immediacy and intuition produce the interiorized image on its way to conceptuality. 'The image thus interiorized in memory (*erinnert*) is no longer *there* [là], no longer existent or present, but preserved in an unconscious dwelling, conserved without consciousness (*bewusstlos, aufbewahrt*). Intelligence keeps these images in reserve, submerged at the bottom of a very dark shelter, like the water in a nightlike or unconscious pit [*comme l'eau d'un puits nocturne* (*nächtliche Schacht*) *ou inconscient* (*bewusstlose Schacht*)]' (77; 88). The sign, the bridge, the middle term (*Mittelpunkt*), the gangway: 'like the water in a nocturnal or unconscious pit'.

17 November 2004. Margaret Hassan has been killed in Iraq. The sign (the bridge as a gap that cannot be bridged) unites the signified and the signifier, but 'Hegel must immediately recognize a kind of separation [*une sorte d'écart*]', a kind of gap in the signifier as it is re-marked by a representation of a representation ('The pit and the pyramid' 81; 94). The *re*-marks the gap. This gap ('like the water in a nocturnal . . . pit') is *already* at the heart of the Hegelian pyramid, of the sign as the body inhabited and animated by the spirit, as the tomb, the *monument*, that 'capitalizes on life [*thésaurise la vie*] by marking that life continues elsewhere . . . It consecrates the disappearance of life by attesting to the perseverance of life' (82; 95). This is the *beginning* of the monu-memorialization of the absent father or mother. The sign (as 'the monument-of-life-in-death, the monument-of-death-in-life [*monument-de-la-vie-dans-la-mort, monu-ment-de-la-mort-dans-la-vie*]') marks at once, *despite itself*, not only the 'work of death [*le travail de la mort*]' in the preservation and the aggrandizement of life (as a pyramid to the proper), but also the *other* of the economy of either life *as* death *or* death *as* life (83; 95). It re-marks the *other* life (the trace of the other) and the *other* death (the wholly other): *life death* (*la vie la mort*).

18 November 2004. How does Hegel get to Plato? In the *Lectures on the History of Philosophy* he must pass *through* 'Oriental Philosophy' (Chinese and Indian philosophies), and he reminds his readers that the Greeks

> certainly received the substantial beginnings [*Anfänge*] of their religion, cul-ture, their common bonds of fellowship, more or less, from Asia, Syria and Egypt; but they have so greatly obliterated the foreign nature of this origin [*aber sie haben das Fremde dieses Ursprungs so sehr getilgt*], and it is so much changed, worked upon, turned round [*umgewandelt, verarbeitet, umgekehrt*], and altogether made so different [*ein Anderes daraus gemacht*], that what they, as we, prize, know, and love in it, is essentially their own. (150; 174)

For Plato and Hegel, writing is an *Egyptian* question and it is a question that takes both Hegel and Derrida to the history of philosophy ('The pit and the pyramid' 99–100; Bennington, 'Mosaic fragment').

An Egyptian *digression* with Herodotus, whom Hegel called a historian without reflection, a historian who does not speculate, who does not play with the dialectic (*The Philosophy of History* 1–2). 'I need not apologize for the digression – it has been my plan throughout this work' (Herodotus, *The Histories* 280, trans. de Selincourt).

'Dissemination would propose a certain theory ... of *digression*' ('Outwork' 27 n. 27).

'What all these professorial procedures with regard to the shoes are lacking in, moreover, is the sense of digression' ('Restitutions' 293).

Herodotus, the master of digressions, understood the gaps between the Hellene and the barbarian, the other *of* the Greeks. Nietzsche also understood the absurdity of this gap as a proper gap, as a gap of propriety: 'And so time after time cordial anger erupts against this presumptuous little people that made bold for all time to designate everything not native as "barbaric"' (*The Birth of Tragedy*, trans. Kaufman, §15).

Western philosophy, biography and history originated not in the West, but in the gangway between the "West" and the "East", in the small boats that sailed from one side of the Bosphorus or the Hellespont to the other and criss-crossed the Aegean. Before Plato built the foundations of Western philosophy within the walls of Athens, there was Thales, Anaximander and Anaximenes of Miletus. Miletus, on the coast of Asia Minor (modern Turkey), was a Greek city-state under the Lydian and Persian empires. Not one of the notable Presocratic philosophers was an Athenian. Heraclitus, Xenophanes and Anaxagoras came from city-states north of Miletus. Pythagoras was born on the island of Samos and spent most of his life in Italy. Parmenides and Zeno were natives of Italy and only Anaxagoras appears to have lived in Athens. Philosophy may have been a Greek concern, but it originated in the gap *between* the Greeks and the so-called barbarians.

Derrida's work may also be a Parisian, European concern (with a long-standing relation to America), but it originates in the gap between France and Algeria, where Derrida was born on *15 July 1930*. Derrida remarks on *22 September 2001* in a paper given in Frankfurt, 'I will pass over all the gaps [*tous les écarts*] of my non-belonging to French culture' (*Fichus: Discours de Francfort* 46).

As Jonathan Barnes observes, 'many of the Greeks themselves believed that philosophy began among 'the barbarians' – in Egypt, in Persia, in Babylonia. They credited the early Presocratics with journeys to Egypt and the Near East, and supposed that they returned with philosophy among their souvenirs' (*Early Greek Philosophers* 58). It is only when the Greeks travel that they find philosophy.

The earliest biographer in the West was probably Skylax of Caryanda, another Greek born in Asia Minor (Momigliano, *The Development of Greek Biography* 29, 36, 44, 104). Herodotus tells us that Skylax led an expedition on behalf of the Persian King Darius down the Indus River and Aristotle records that he wrote an account of his travels in India (285; *Politics* 1332b). Herodotus – not the first historian in the West but, as Cicero called him, *pater historiae*, the 'Father of History' – was born in Halicarnassus, south of Miletus (*De Legibus* 1.1.3–5). Given the probability that the origins of Western philosophy, biography and history are to be found at the point where Greece came into contact with the East, it is appropriate that Herodotus devotes his researches (*historia*) to preserving 'the memory of the past by putting on record the astonishing achievements both of our own and of other peoples; and more particularly, to show how they came into conflict' (41 [1: 1]). Herodotus had the rare virtue in ancient Greece of taking account of the customs, traditions and achievements of the barbarians (Momigliano, 'The place of Herodotus in the history of historiography'; Hartog, *The Mirror of Herodotus*). It is no small thing that in the opening words of *The Histories* he says that he wants to put 'on record the *astonishing* achievements *both* of our own *and of other peoples*' (trans. de Selincourt 41), 'those great and wonderful deeds, manifested by *both* Greeks and barbarians [*barbároisi*]' (trans. Grene 33).

Perhaps the most remarkable example of Herodotus's willingness to inquire into the traditions of the barbarians is his account of the Egyptian version of the greatest of Greek epic stories, the kidnapping of Helen and the siege of Troy (trans. de Selincourt 170–4 [2: 112–20]). Travelling in Egypt, Herodotus discovers a temple in Memphis that may have been 'built in honour of Helen'. Questioning the priests in the temple, he is told that it is believed that bad weather had forced Paris to land in Egypt 'with his stolen bride'. The 'Trojan stranger' was then brought before the Pharaoh who tells him:

> If . . . I did not consider it a matter of great importance that I have never yet put to death any stranger who has been forced upon my coasts by stress of weather, I should have punished you for the sake of your Greek host. To be welcomed as a guest, and to repay that kindness by so foul a deed! You are a villain. You seduced your friend's wife, and, as if that were not enough, persuaded her to escape with you on the wings of passion you roused. Even that did not content you – but you must bring with you besides the treasure you have stolen from your host's house. But though I cannot punish a stranger with death, I will not allow you to take away your ill-gotten gains. I will keep this woman and the treasure, until the Greek to whom they belong chooses to come and fetch them.

The priests tell Herodotus that even though the Trojans insisted that Helen was not in Troy, the Greeks persisted with their siege and it was only after the city fell that Meneleus came to Egypt to find his wife. At Pharaoh's court Meneleus was

> most hospitably entertained and Helen, none the worse for her adventures, was restored to him with all the rest of his property. Nevertheless, in spite of this generous treatment, Meneleus proved himself no friend to Egypt; for when he wished to leave, but was delayed for a long time by contrary winds, he took two Egyptian children and offered them in sacrifice.

In the Egyptian account of the kidnapping of Helen, it is not the collective arms of the Greeks, but the Pharaoh who, while honouring the ancient laws of hospitality, restores the 'stolen bride' to her husband. Even more extraordinary is the account of Meneleus's behaviour in Egypt. Echoing his brother Agamemnon's fateful decision, as Aeschylus says, to 'put on the harness of Necessity' and to sacrifice Iphigenia (*Agamemnon* 217–18), Meneleus responds to the faultless propriety of the Egyptians by transgressing the basic rules of hospitality. The Greeks are not good guests.

It is hard to imagine an equivalent epic narrative that is more inextricably tied to the identity of a people than the stories related in the *Odyssey* and the *Iliad*. The Romans were sufficiently envious of the Greeks to claim that the founder of Rome had fought at Troy, while being careful to ensure that he was a Trojan and not a Greek (Momigliano, 'How to reconcile Greeks and Trojans'). Herodotus's record of the Egyptian version of the kidnapping of Helen gives the barbarian an authoritative and dignified role in this most precious, most iconic, of Greek epics. Such an unchecked authority about Greek names would have alarmed Socrates and it is unsurprising that Herodotus was attacked by Plutarch in his essay 'On the malice of Herodotus' for being 'pro-barbarian'. Plutarch insists that Herodotus tells 'worthless Egyptian stories to overthrow the most solemn and sacred truths of Greek religion' and that he is 'a malicious liar', because he repeats 'unworthy and false notions about the greatest and best cities and men of Greece' (XI: 13, 25, 43).

For his part, in his *Lives* Plutarch faithfully represents Greek anxieties about the barbarian in the *agora*. Because his mother was not an Athenian, Themistocles was educated at the gymnasium of Cynosarges, the school for those of 'mixed or alien parentage' which stands outside of the city walls. Nonetheless, Plutrarch notes, Themistocles was able to persuade 'a number of young men of good family to go out to Cynosarges and take their exercise with him, and by this ingenious social manoeuvre he is believed to have done away with the discrimination between pure Athenians and those of mixed descent' ('Themistocles' 77). Despite this apparent victory, Plutarch records that Pericles later passed a law 'that only those who could claim Athenian parentage on both sides should be counted as Athenian citizens'. As a result of this law, some five thousand 'impure' Athenians were sold into slavery ('Pericles' 203–4).

The fear of 'becoming barbarized' by their Eastern neighbours played a significant role in bringing to an end the brief and unlamented empire of the Greeks ('Lysander' 289). As Gibbon observed, 'the narrow policy of preserving, without any foreign mixture, the pure blood of the ancient citizens, had checked the fortune, and hastened the ruin, of Athens and Sparta'. In contrast to the Greek city-states, Gibbon writes, 'the aspiring genius of Rome sacrificed vanity to ambition, and deemed it more prudent, as well as honourable, to adopt virtue and merit for her own wheresoever they were found, among slaves or strangers, enemies or barbarians' (I: 61). In his *Histories*, Herodotus of Halicarnassus, who spent his last years far from Athens as a citizen of Thuria in Italy, has Xerxes say, 'the relationship between men of different countries is very different from that between men of the same town; a man is full of sympathy for the good fortune of a foreign friend' (523 [7: 237]). He also records the words of the Spartan envoys to Athens: 'for surely you know that in foreigners there is neither truth nor honour' (574 [8: 142]).

19 November 2004. 'Or if one prefers, here Hegel's formula must be taken literally: history is nothing but the history of philosophy, absolute knowledge is fulfilled' (*Of Grammatology* 286). For Hegel, logic (as a progressive deduction of the forms of the pure Idea) and history (as a progression of the particular stages of the empirical form in time) are of the *same* order: 'the study of the history of philosophy is the study of philosophy itself'. If one 'entirely divested [*entkleidet*]' history of its relation to the particular, the external and the empirical it would become philosophy. History is 'the development of the idea in the empirical, external form'. History is the body (as time, in time). Philosophy is the spirit (as truth, in truth) (*Lectures* 29–30; 49). To be alive, to be animated, to be itself, history can *only* be a history of philosophy. As Jean Hyppolite noted, 'only spirit has a history, that is, a development of itself by itself such that it retains its identity in each of its particularizations'. Only the spirit is 'a concrete whole which, consequently, has a novel development and a real history'. Only spirit can give the *Aufhebung* and the *Erinnerung to* history, can give meaning to history (*Genesis and Structure* 33, 37).

'What Hegel,' Derrida writes in 'The pit and the pyramid', 'the *relevant* interpreter of the entire history of philosophy, *could never think* is a machine that would work [*fonctionnerait*]' without the work of the negative '*presenting* itself [*se* présenter] . . . in the service of meaning'. Hegel could not think of a machine 'that would work without, to this extent, being governed by an order of reappropriation [*qui fonctionnerait sans être* . . . that would work without being . . .]' (107; 126).

Écarts as a machine, as a gap machine that separates, moves apart, distances: machines for travelling – for cars (*écartement des essieux*, wheelbase), for trains (*écartement des rails*, rail gauge) – and for operations (*écarteur*, retractor). Machines that do not *turn back*, that do not take the wheels away from the car or the tracks away from the train, or close the open, the gaping wound: machines without 'a circle returning within itself' (*Lectures* 27).

Écarts: producing 'a machine by introducing a disparity or gap [*un écart*] in the customary use of discourse' ('Psyche: Inventions of the other' 43; 35). *Écarts*: 'an event machine [*un événement-machine*]' – 'a machinelike repetition *and* that which happens/arrives [*une répétition machinale* et *ce qui arrive*]'. An 'event machine' as the possibility of the event ('Typewriter ribbon' 73, 136; 36, 115). An 'event machine' for a history of gaps, for writing after *8–9 October 2004*.

21 November 2004.   A friend gave me a book when I was in Paris last month, *Biographie de la faim* (2004) by Amélie Nothomb. Nothomb writes about being a diplomat's daughter, of a childhood of displacement, of rapacious hunger and self-imposed starvation, of a childhood of digressions and of diplomacy *as* displacement. For the eight-year-old Belgian girl attending a New York ballet school, 'the first stage was the splits [*la première étape était le grand écart*]' (114). All eight-year-old girls should be able to *begin* with the splits she is told, and without too much difficulty she is able to do the 'hoped-for split [*l'écart espéré*]' (115). She is able to do it without difficulty and is still astonished ('*étonnement de voir ses jambes en compas autour de soi*'). She has to *start* with *le grand écart*. She hopes for it and, on her first attempt, she succeeds and succeeds in *astonishing* herself. This could be a narrative for Derrida's reading of Hegel.

Le grand écart: it almost sounds like the title of a film noir from the 1940s – *The Big Sleep, Le Grand Écart, The Big Separation*. 'Can death be reduced . . . to a separation [*à un partage*]?' Derrida asks in *Aporias* (1992–1996) (6; 22). For Derrida, death *cannot* be reduced to *The Big Separation* because this is what Plato fears – 'the attempt at universal separation [*dialúein*] is the final annihilation of all reasoning' (*Sophist* 259e) – and what Hegel (on his way to Plato) at first succeeds in doing – 'and the greater power overcomes the greater separation [*Ausdehnung*]' (*Lectures* 28; 47) – and then (as Derrida never stops reminding us) *astonishes* himself.

22 November 2004. Three separations in English, three kinds of separation in translation: *partage, dialúein, Ausdehnung*. 'This border does not pass among various languages. It separates [*sépare*] translatability within one and the same language . . . Babelization does not therefore wait for the multiplicity of languages. The identity of the language can only affirm itself as identity to itself by opening itself to the hospitality of a difference from itself or of a difference with itself', *Aporias* (10; 28).

Littré, that great resource for Derrida of *les sources écartées*, suggests that the French word *écart* is already a kind of translation. *Écart* is Spanish in origin (*scarto*) and first appears in French in the early seventeenth century as a '*terme de jeu*': when playing cards, cards are discarded (*les cartes écartées*), one discards (*écart aux cartes*). *Écarts* are always a game of chance, a throw of the dice. What else can they be when one is dealing with gaps? What have I left out? What have I missed? *The gaps*! *Le Robert*, on the other hand, suggests that *écart* is a French word and first appears in the thirteenth century meaning distance, space or gap.

According to the *OED* the word gap in English has its origins (in the plural) in the Old Norse for chasm, which is related to *gapa* (to gape) and to *gab* (an open mouth, an opening) in Danish. *Gap* is also a Swedish word. Gape (*gapa*) can also be related to the Dutch *gapen* and to the German *gaffen*. In all these languages, the gap is the gaping opening, the wound that cannot be closed. Gap-gapa-gab-gapen-gaffen: an impossible mourning.

Of course, there is also *The Gap*, the American *Gap*, the gap to *close* a gap in the market, the capitalization of the gap as a series of international outlet shops where "the gap" is always the same, no matter what language. It is a gap that has no need of translation, that appears to efface its own babelization. And there are the British gaps that one can never avoid when travelling by train or by tube in London: 'Mind the Gap', a recorded voice will say as you step over the abyss, without a gangway, from platform to machine. To travel in England, one must *mind the gap*. Everywhere, they are telling you: *mind the gap*. And this is all that I am trying to do; to mind the gaps that the life and death of Jacques Derrida have left behind, have left before us and in front of us. 'One must untangle [*démêler*] all these threads and respect all these strata and discrepancies [*ces décalages*]' ('Plato's pharmacy' 144 n. 68; 180 n. 63).

Mind the gaps.

In German, there are many gaps: *die Öffnung, Lücke, Kluft, Spalt, Riß, Sprung, Scharte, Unterbrechung, Unterschied. Unterscheiden* means to discriminate, to separate, to differentiate, to differ (one could almost add, *to gap*). In both 'différance' and '*Ousia* and *Grammē*' (1968) Derrida, quotes an untranslated passage from Heidegger's 'Anaximander's saying' (1946):

> Heidegger also says that difference [and the gap] cannot appear *as such* [comme telle]: "*Lichtung des Unterschiedes kann deshalb auch nicht bedeuten, dass der Unterschied als der Unterschied erscheint* ['Illumination of the difference, therefore, cannot mean that the difference appears as the difference' (275)]." There is no essence of *différance*; it (is) that which not only could never be appropriated in the *as such* [comme tel] of its name or its appearing, but also which threatens the authority of the *as such* [comme tel] in general, of the presence of the thing itself in its essence. ('Différance' 25–6 [27]; see also '*Ousia* and *Grammē*' 66 [77])

For Husserl, the *as such* is the essence of generality, generality as essence (*Ideas I* 52). Heidegger will later write that 'thinking as such [*als solches*]' is what Hegel does (*Identity and Difference* 42; 107). The gap *as such* is a gap that *only* opens to *close* itself. The possibility of the *as such* for Heidegger, Derrida will argue in *Aporias*, is the possibility of speech, of 'death *as* death', of the proper, of what the animal cannot do (35–7, 71–6, 78).

How can there be a *narrative* of gaps? How can there be a narrative of gaps that are not simply gaps *as such*? How can there be a narrative *of* gaps? How can there be a narrative *with* gaps, with all these digressions and translations? How does one mourn for Jacques Derrida, without closing the gap?

Perhaps with the *date*, with the finitude of the date, with the text as a series of dates, with the unforeseeable *event* of the date: *22 November 2004*.

Perhaps with the *restance* (the remainder that always remains to come) of the *incomplete*.

In 'Aporias', first given as a paper on *15 July 1992* (Derrida's birthday) at Cerisy-la-Salle, Derrida writes of 'the essential incompleteness of translating' (9). And one could describe his reading of Husserl's *The Origin of Geometry* as an attempt to mark the difference (the almost nothing) between the *incomplete* as the *infinite* (phenomenology as a virtual presence, as anticipation, horizon and teleology, as the 'anticipated unity in every incompletion', 117) and the *incomplete* as the *indefinite* (as writing, as *différance*, as the possibility and the ruin of phenomenology). It is through Husserl's ultimate reliance on Kant that Derrida begins to trace this movement and it is hardly fortuitous that Kant *begins* the *Critique of Pure Reason* with the problem of the incomplete.

Human reason, Kant writes in the preface – and again it is a question of the *pre-* – to the first edition (1781) is 'burdened with questions which it cannot dismiss', but which it 'also cannot answer' (A vii). It is because reason 'begins from principles' that are determined by *experience* that it encounters unanswerable questions that 'transcend every capacity of human reason'. The more its principles are dictated by experience, the more reason goes beyond 'the bounds of all experience'. When reason starts *from* experience reason is driven into the unanswerable. Reason 'becomes aware . . . that its business must always remain incomplete [*unvollendet*] because the questions never cease' (A viii). Starting from experience, reason is 'put into dissension with itself' and, no longer able to 'recognize any touchstone in experience', loses itself in 'groundless pretensions' (A viii, A xi–xii). Kant responds to this problem of the incomplete with the 'perfect unity [*vollkommene Einheit*]' of pure reason. Pure reason can answer all the questions 'set for it by its own nature'. Relying on 'pure concepts', it has 'unconditioned completeness [*unbedingte Vollständigkeit*]' (A xiii, A xx).

Hegel *begins* with the lingering incompletion in the Kantian *a priori*: 'However much Philosophy . . . is *a priori*, it is at the same time just as really a result, since the thought produced and, indeed, the life and action are produced to produce themselves' (*Lectures* 51). According to Hegel, for philosophy to be complete, it must *produce* itself. The *a priori* is always in need of the *Aufhebung* – and the *Aufhebung* can never escape *différance*.

23 November 2004. *A digression* ('I need not apologize for the digression – it has been my plan throughout this work'). Plutarch could never forgive Herodotus, the father of history, for suggesting that the Egyptians could be better hosts than the Greeks. 'The host must hurry [*l'hote doit se hater*]',

Derrida says on *17 January 1996* in his lectures on hospitality (*Of Hospitality* 123; 109, trans. modified). Hospitality is always a matter of urgency, always a question of *speeds*. The unexpected guests arrive and there is always a rush of activity: a hurried welcoming at the door, a quick cleaning up, a surreptitious rearranging or putting back into order, a preparing of food and drink. But even when the guest is expected, has been expected for a long time, there is a sense of urgency. The guests arrive – always too early or too late, even if they are "on time". Coats are taken; tours are given of the immaculate, impossibly ordered home; drinks are served, food presented. For there to be a place for hospitality, for hospitality to take (the) place, *the host must hurry*.

As Derrida has suggested in *The Gift of Death* (1992), *Adieu* (1997), *Of Hospitality* (1997) and 'Hostpitality' (1997), for the peoples of the Book, for the three great Abrahamic descendants – Jews, Christians and Muslims – hospitality begins with *Genesis* 18:1–9. Abraham is 'sitting at the entrance to his tent at the heat of the day' when he sees three men:

> When he saw them, he ran to meet them from the entrance to
> his tent and bowed to the earth
> and said:
> My lords,
> pray if I have found favour in your eyes,
> pray do not pass by your servant!
> Pray let a little water be fetched, then wash your feet and recline
> under the tree;
> let me fetch (you) a bit of bread, that you may refresh your
> hearts,
> then afterward you may pass on –
> for you have, after all, passed your servant's way!
> They said:
> Do thus, as you have spoken.
> Avraham hastened into his tent to Sara and said:
> Make haste! (*Genesis* 18:1–6, *The Five Books of Moses*, Fox trans.)

As Kierkegaard observed, 'what is omitted from Abraham's story is the anxiety', and in this instance the anxiety to be hospitable as quickly as he can (*Fear and Trembling* 28). Running out to meet the three travellers, Abraham rushes back to his tent and says to Sara: 'Make haste! [*Mahari*].' When it comes to Abrahamic hospitality, there is never enough time. No matter how fast you run, the gap between the host and the guest can never be bridged. From 'sitting . . . at the heat of the day', suddenly, there is not enough time for Abraham to run and to entreat the travellers to accept water and food. There is not enough time to hear their command to receive hospitality ('Do thus, as you have spoken') and, already, not enough time for Abraham to say 'Make haste!' to Sara.

And Abraham keeps running, keeps saying, make haste:

> Avraham hastened into his tent to Sara and said:
> Make haste! Three measures of choice flour! Knead it, make
> bread-cakes!
> Avraham ran to the oxen,
> he fetched a young ox, tender and fine, and gave it to a
> serving-lad, that he might hasten to make it ready;
> then he fetched cream and milk and the young ox that he had
> made ready, and placed it before them. (18:6–8)

It is only when water to bathe the travellers' feet has been brought, when the bread-cakes to refresh their hearts have been made, and when cream and milk and meat have been placed 'before them', that there is enough time and Abraham can stop running and stop commanding others to hasten: 'Now he stood over against them under the tree while they ate' (18:8).

Genesis 18 opens with an unexpected visitation for Abraham. 'Now YHWH was seen by him by the oaks of Mamre as he was sitting at the entrance of his tent at the heat of the day' (18:1). For the sages of the *Talmud*, this visitation *without any possible hospitality* is the *origin* of Abrahamic hospitality. Hospitality begins with an impossible hospitality.

> Why did God make that day very hot? R. Hama bar Hanina explained: It was the third day after Abraham's circumcision [when he was particularly weak], and the Holy One came to ask how Abraham was; so He drew the sun out of its sheath [to make the day so hot], that the righteous Abraham would not be troubled by attending to wayfarers. [Since no one came because of the heat.] Abraham sent out Eliezer [to look around]. He went out but found no wayfarers. So, in accord with the proverb 'Never trust a slave,' Abraham said, 'I do not believe you,' and he himself went out. 'And he lifted up his eyes, and looked, and lo, three men stood by him' (Gen. 18:2). What kind of people were these three [who were able to stir abroad on such a hot day]? They were the angels Michael, Raphael, and Gabriel. (Bialik and Ravnitzky *The Book of Legends* 35: 26)

According to R. Hama bar Hanina, God, the visitor that one never expects and that one always waits for, makes the day 'so hot' to spare Abraham the burden of being hospitable to wayfarers. Abraham is so anxious that he is not being hospitable, that he might miss the chance of *offering* hospitality that, weak as he is, he still goes out into the heat of the day and meets the three angels. God prevents Abraham, who is always rushing to be hospitable, from wearing himself out on the wrong guests. God does not temper or slow down Abraham's haste to host, he just ensures that the right guests come at the right time.

There is something excessive, almost mad about Abraham's urgent need to run out in the midday sun and find someone to host. Abraham sits at the door of his tent, staring out into the desert under a blinding sun, waiting to run, to ambush, to kidnap some passer-by and make them an offer they cannot refuse. To be hospitable, Derrida observes, is to become *at once* the host (*l'hôte*) *or* the guest (*l'hôte*) *and* the hostage of the other (*Adieu* 116; 200). Even God seems unable to control this mad precipitation towards the wandering other, this rush to take the other into one's home, to become a hostage of the other. God relies on this mad, uncontrollable, speed of Abrahamic hospitality.

For R. Hanina, it is important that Abraham runs out into the sun and only *then* finds the impossible travellers. Prompted by a visitation that exceeds any possible hospitality, hospitality begins with a mad rush into the *empty* desert, with an impossible hospitality for *anyone and no one*. But while R. Hanina insists that Abraham runs out of his tent and *then* sees the wayfarers, the *Torah* is more circumspect about this scene:

> Now YHWH was seen by him by the oaks of Mamre
> as he was sitting at the entrance of his tent at the heat of the day.
> He lifted up his eyes and saw:
> here, three men standing over against him.
> When he saw them, he ran to meet them from the entrance to
> the tent and bowed to the earth. (18:1–2)

Abraham has not simply run out into the sun, rushing to meet anyone and no one. The offer of a universal anonymous hospitality, of hospitality without check, of speeding without brakes, always risks the mirages of the desert, risks the phantom of a wayfarer. But isn't an angel a kind of phantom wayfarer? According to the *Torah*, Abraham has sat 'at the entrance to his tent' and it is *only* when, out of nowhere, the three men (the three angels) appear that he then runs 'to meet them from the entrance of the tent'. Abraham *waits* and then he runs. He only runs when he sees that he can offer his hospitality to *someone* and he only runs when he can rush *across* the entrance of his own tent and meet the travellers. It is only when first seeing the potential guests from *within* the shade of his own tent (his *chez soi*), and then *leaving* his domain *for* their sake, that he can be hospitable. The *Torah* says don't go too fast, delay a moment, take a look at who is out there – and then run as fast as you can, and never stop running *for* the other.

'But what did Abraham do?' Kierkegaard asks. 'He arrived neither too early nor too late' (*Fear and Trembling* 35). On Mount Moriah, Abraham has the timing right. Now, waiting at the threshold of his tent, can Abraham have the timing right? Is there a right timing for hospitality? R. Hanina's hospitality is an *absolute* hospitality, a hospitality without the indeterminacy of a slowing down becoming a speeding up *and* a speeding up becoming a slowing down, a hospitality without the impossible demand of *speeds* (traces of *différance*). As the *Torah* suggests, Abraham waits, he sees three men in the desert, he runs out and makes his case, pleads his cause for hospitality and runs back, commands everyone to rush and – by chance, by luck, by the power of his eloquence, by waiting and then going as fast as he can – he is able to host the wayfarers, to be hospitable. It is only the delay – the waiting *at* the threshold, the crossing *of* the threshold – that makes the running and rushing *to* the other and *for* the other, the injunction to make haste, possible. Hospitality is always a question of more than one of speed, of speeds.

At the most crucial moment when he is pleading his case, begging to be allowed to offer his hospitality, why does Abraham only say that he will bring 'a little water' and 'a bit of bread'? 'Righteous men,' the *Talmud* comments, 'say little but perform much' (547: 108). Abraham offers a little water and bread, then brings a banquet. But this is also a matter of the speeds of hospitality. Abraham runs from his tent, bows to the earth and brings the travellers to a *stop*. He *detains* the wayfarers by falling to the ground and saying:

> My lords,
> pray if I have found favour in your eyes,
> pray do not pass by your servant!

In this first scene of hospitality for the Abrahamic faiths, after *waiting* and *running*, there is the attempt to *detain*: to keep or hold back a passer-by from passing on. Abraham doesn't have much time to convince the travellers not to pass on, to promise that he will *not* detain them for too long from their journey and their destination. Abrahamic hospitality is an interruption, a deviation from the destination. The act of hospitality is the urgent attempt to detain with a promise that there will be no *detention*. Hospitality to the passing stranger must promise the briefest of delays, the shortest of detours. Hospitality, like life, can only be offered with the assurance that 'afterwards you may pass on':

> pray do not *pass* by your servant!
> Pray let a *little* water be fetched, then wash your feet and recline
> under the tree;
> let me fetch (you) a *bit* of bread, that you may refresh your
> hearts,
> then afterward you may *pass on*

In the *Talmud*, R. Joshua bar Hanquiah makes much of the fact that Abraham acts as a servant to the travellers. He both serves the food to them himself and remains standing while they eat. When Abraham commands Sara to use 'three measures of choice flour!' to make the bread-cakes, R. Isaac interprets the emphasis on 'choice flour' as a sign 'that a woman is more apt than a man to be stingy with guests' (626: 132). For R. Isaac, true hospitality, the hospitality that – without hesitation – gives the best to the guest or the stranger, is the hospitality *of* Abraham: Abraham alone is the servant. But there can be no Abrahamic hospitality without Sara and the other servants. The *first* thing Abraham does is run to Sara and shout 'Make haste!' The speeds of hospitality begin with both Abraham and Sara. Abraham shouts out 'Make haste!' and Sara makes haste. *Between* Abraham shouting out and Sara hastening anything can happen: the uncertain, immeasurable speeds of hospitality have started. 'He or she, if the interruption of the discourse is required' (Derrida, 'At this very moment in this work here I am' 18). Was Sarah in time? The *Torah* makes no mention of the bread-cakes again or who delivers them or how long it takes to bring them. Did Sara delay cooking the bread? Did she rush and overcook them because Abraham had run into the tent from the midday sun like a madman, crying out, 'Make haste!'? Whatever Abraham himself does, the *first* question the travellers ask when they are eating is, 'Where is Sara your wife?' (18:9).

R. Joshua goes on to ask, 'Do you suppose that his guests appeared to him openly as ministering angels? They appeared to him disguised as mere Arabs' (220: 79). This anachronistic observation – it is Abraham's first son Ishmael who will become the father of the Arabs – emphasizes that all of Abraham's anxiety and urgency, all of the speeds of hospitality in this first scene of Abrahamic hospitality, is devoted to 'mere Arabs', to the other, to the other who, as a 'ministering angel', will promise the birth of a long-hoped-for son with Sara. In this first scene of hospitality for Jews, Christians and Muslims – after God has invited Adam and Eve to the Garden of Eden and Noah has invited the animals into the Ark – Abraham is always running *after* the other, running *for* the other. There is always a gap when it comes to hospitality. There is *never enough time* to be hospitable, *truly* hospitable, to the other: the Abrahamic inheritance.

24 November 2004. In *Spurs: Nietzsche's Styles* (1972–1978) Derrida uses *écartement* (divergence) as part of his retranslation of *Entfernung* (distance, departure; *entfernen* – to move away, wander, withdraw). In *Being and Time* Heidegger creates a gap in *Ent-fernung*, a gap *for Dasein*. 'Dasein is essentially not a Being-present-at-hand', he writes, and 'cannot signify anything like occurrence at a position in "world-space" '. *Dasein* cannot be simply close or merely far away (H104–5). *Ent-Fernung* is the *withdrawal* that removes or reverses distance to create *proximity*. Macquarrie and Robinson translate it as *de-severance*. In *Spurs*, tracing the strange relation in Nietzsche's texts between "woman", and "truth", Derrida writes:

> If it is necessary to keep one's distance from the feminine operation . . . it is perhaps because "the woman" ["*la femme*"] is not some thing, the determinable identity which announces itself from a distance, at a distance from some other thing, from which it would withdrawal or approach. Perhaps she is, as a non-identity, a non-figure, a simulacrum, the *abîme* of distance, the out-distancing of distance, the interval's cadence [*la coupe de l'espacement*, the cut, the gap of spacing], distance itself, if one can still say this, which is impossible, distance *itself*. Distance out-distances itself, the far is furthered. One is forced to appeal here to the Heideggerian use of the word *Entfernung*: at once the divergence [*l'écartement*], the distance [*l'éloignement*] and the distantiation of distance [*l'éloignement de l'éloignement*], the deferment of the distant [*lointain*], the de-ferment [*l'é-loignement*], it is in fact the destruction (*Ent-*) which constitutes the distant as such [*comme tel*], the veiled enigma of proximation. (48–51, trans. modified)

In retranslating *Ent-fernung* as *l'é-loignement*, Derrida starts with the gap of spacing (*la coupe de l'espacement*), the gap as *spacing*, that 'other sense of *différer'*, of *différance* – of differing *and* deferring as space becoming time and time becoming space ('Différance' 8). The *spacing* of the cut, of the gap as spacing, marks the cadence, the rhythm of *différance* as the possibility *and* the limitation of closeness, proximity and propriety.

As Derrida suggests in 'Pas' (1976–1986), from the start the 'strange "pas" [step, not] of *é-loignement'* gathers and distances *propriety* (the propriety of both *the* near and *the* far), without the proper having the time, or the space, to be itself (28, 31). Propriety – the very possibility of the presence of the present – 'is structurally in withdrawal as divergence [*en retrait comme écart*]' ('The retrait of metaphor' 124).

On *4 September 1997* in *Counterpath* (1999), Derrida returns (but has he ever left) to Heidegger's use of *Ent-fernung* for *Dasein*:

> The existence of the *Dasein* could basically be said to tend to approximate closely what is close [*se rapprocher du proche*], it tends toward *rapprochement*, proximity (*auf Nähe*). Its first, and therefore last, movement would develop – even when it moves away – *in view of* an approaching, one could perhaps say, "in view of seeing itself come." For that very reason, it would depend on an experience of *é-loignement*, on the distancing of distancing. *Ent-Fernung / Näherung*. But doesn't distancing *from* and *in* distancing, distancing as *rapprochement*, approximation, reappropriation, still remain within Ulysses's circle? Not that every traverse is *necessarily* an Odyssey, but the phantasmic logic of the Odyssey remains all powerful. Unless it hits the snag [*Sauf à buter*] (54–5; 57).

Hitting a snag: the gap that *moves*.

25 November 2005. At the invitation of Joanna Hodge I am going to Manchester today to give a long-planned paper in the Department of Philosophy at Manchester Metropolitan University on Derrida and *life death*, which has now become a private *and* public (somewhere in between) speaking on Derrida and *la vie la mort*, before *and* after (somewhere in between) the death of Jacques Derrida: an impossible mourning.

26 November 2004. *Écarts*: 'the work exceeds itself, it surpasses the limits of the concept of itself that it claims to have properly while presenting itself' *Aporias* (32). When on *12 October* I began writing, when I began with the last paragraph of Derrida's 1959 paper on Husserl, when I began with the *precedant* that goes first, that takes pre-cedence and gives up its place, goes on ahead, that predeceases, the *arrivant* of *Aporias* was not far away. The *arrivant* evokes 'the neutrality of *that which* arrives, but also the singularity of *who* arrives, he or she who comes, coming to where she or he was not expected, where one was awaiting him or her without waiting for him or her, without expecting it [*s'y attendre*]' (33).

Nor was Derrida's questioning of Heidegger's claim of precedence via a certain hedgehog (*Ick bünn all hier*, I am already here) that far away, a claim in which 'the *Da* or the *Fort-Da* of *Dasein* would belong to this "logic" of destination that permits one to say, everywhere and always "I have always already arrived at the destination [*je suis toujours déjà arrivé à destination*]" ': a precedence without pre-cedence (*Identity and Difference* 63; 'Istrice 2. Ick bünn all hier' 304; 314). As Catherine Malabou writes of Derrida's work at the opening of 'L'écartement des voies' ('The parting of the ways'): '*Arriving* and *deriving* have separated. *Catastrophe* is the name for the parting [*écart*] that henceforth keeps each out of range of the other. "Henceforth" means since Derrida has passed by, since he has situated the very possibility of the *voyage* within that space or parting [*en cet écart ou cet écartement*]' (*Counterpath* 1; 11). Voyaging in the gaps.

But I had forgotten the precedence of pre-cede in *Aporias*:

> The *s'attendre* that I have used in order to translate Heidegger's sentence involves imminence, indeed, the anxious anticipation of something, but also the double or rather triple transitivity (non-reflexive and reflexive) of the expecting, the waiting for *something* that will happen as the completely other than oneself, but of waiting (for each other) by awaiting oneself also, by preceding oneself as if one had a meeting with a oneself that one is but does not know [*en précédent soi-même comme si on avait rendez-vous avec un soi-même qu'on est et qu'on ne connaît pas*]. The German sentence says, "*Mit dem Tod steht sich das Dasein selbst in seinem eigensten Seinkönnen bevor.*" Martineau translates *steht bevor* by *se pré-cède* ("*Avec la mort, le Dasein se pré-cède lui-même en son pouvoir-être le plus propre*"; with death Dasein pre-cedes itself in is most proper being-able). Vezen translates *steht bevor* by a *rendez-vous* . . . Macquarrie and Robinson remind us of another connotation of being-before-itself when they translate it more literally by "stands before itself" . . . With death, *Dasein* is indeed *in front of* itself, *before* itself [devant *lui-même*, avant *lui-même*] (*bevor*), both as before [*devant*] a mirror and as before [*devant*] the future: it awaits itself, it precedes itself [*se précède*], it has a rendezvous with itself. (66; 118–19)

To pre-cede oneself: a rendezvous 'with a oneself that one is but does not know', 'waiting for *something* that will happen as the completely other than oneself'.

I am always pre-ceded – in the end.

28 November 2004.   Death is 'always too soon [*toujours trop tôt*] or too late, untimely [*contretemps*]', Derrida writes in *Aporias* (78; 136). *A digression*. In 1796 Kant had written, 'death always arrives too soon for us'. In the short essay, 'On the power of the mind to master its morbid feelings by sheer resolution', which became the third part of *The Conflict of Faculties*, Kant reflects on *procrastination* in old age, which 'brings with it the habit of postponing [*Vertagung*] important decisions – just as we put off concluding our lives: death always arrives too soon for us [*Todes ist, welcher sich immer zu früh für uns anmeldet*], and we are inexhaustible in thinking up excuses for making it wait' (313; 371). Procrastinating to delay death, we *also* delay and 'put off' the decisions of life; we put off life.

From the *Phaedo* onwards, philosophy has been a kind of death, a virtual death that attempts to exclude the living body from thinking and always has to contend with that *other* death: the always unexpected death of the body. For Kant, the work of philosophy is the labour of '*putting off* [Vertagung]' (314; 373). '*Philosophizing* . . . is a means of warding off [*Abwehrung*]' (317; 377).

For Kant, philosophy is a *regimen*, a rule, a prescribed course, for preventing illness through the 'sheer power of man's reason [*Macht der Vernunft*] to master his sensuous feelings [*Gefühle*] by a self-imposed principle' and Kant uses *himself* as an example of this – a hardy, busy, focused old man who does not oversleep and likes his head and his feet to be cold (316; 375). Philosophy, he suggests, can promise you a long, if somewhat chilly, life.

'The exact opposite of the mind's power to master its pathological feelings', Kant writes, 'is *hypochondria*, the weakness of abandoning oneself despondently to general morbid feelings that have no definite object [*ohne ein bestimmtes Objekt*]' (318; 378). Hypochondria is 'a creature of the imagination [*Geschöpf der Einbildungskraft*]'. It is a '*fictitious* [dichtende] disease', 'a kind of insanity'. *Without a definite object*, 'the patient' becomes a 'self-tormentor [*Selbstquäler*]' prey to the power of the 'inventive imagination [*dichtenden Einbildungskraft*]'. Hypochondria can only be put off, warded off when a 'reasonable human being' asks 'whether his anxiety has an object' and finding that there is no object 'he goes on, despite this claim of his inner feeling [*inneren Gefühls*], to his agenda for the day [*Tagesordnung*]' (318; 378–9). Philosophy wards off the *indefinite* object; it gets on with the business of *today*.

Kant notes that hypochondria is often caused by reading. The reader 'finds in himself symptoms of every disease he reads about in books'.

In this sense, that great reader of books, Don Quixote, can be described as the hypochondriac *par excellence*. As Cervantes had recognized at the beginning of the seventeenth century, literature – which has 'no business to go begging sentences of philosophers, passages of holy writ, poetical fables, rhetorical orations, or miracles of saints' – is an *impossible* 'imitation' of nature, a fiction about fictions, a fiction about what cannot 'fall under the punctuality and preciseness of truth' (*Don Quixote* 20).

Hypochondria is a disease of fictions. So, imagine that Kant, keeping his feet and his head cold as a precaution, is reading Coleridge's 'Dejection: An Ode', first published in 1802 (*Poems* 307–11). Coleridge, Kant might say, is sick. Coleridge's romanticism, and perhaps Romanticism in general, if there is such a thing, is a kind of sickness.

A storm is coming and the narrator in Coleridge's poem wishes 'that even now the gust were swelling'. He *yearns* for the storm that has not come in the hope that it 'might startle this dull pain, and make it move and live!' He *longs* for the external world to 'startle', to shock the internal world into life. An 'unimpassioned grief' has brought the internal world to a state of inertia. Longing for the world outside of him to come to his aid, the narrator still recognizes that he 'may not hope from outward forms to win / The passion and the life, whose fountains are within'. No relief can come from outside. There is *no* definite object in the external world that can help this self-tormentor reach and express the life, the creation, the creativity, within. Of course, we know that there was a definite object for Coleridge: Sara Hutchinson. But it is precisely the complete inaccessibility of Sara Hutchinson that reinforces the absence of a definite object.

'Make haste!' Abraham had called out to the first Sara, she who was neither simply near nor far, neither simply fast nor slow, and always, driving Nietzsche slightly mad, somewhere in between.

For Coleridge, it is both terrible and wonderful that 'in our life alone does nature live'. Life relies entirely on an internal world that the narrator cannot reach. The 'shaping spirit of Imagination' – this 'sweet and potent voice', 'this strong music', 'this light, this glory / This beautiful and beauty-making power' – has failed. Coleridge's poem is a poem of *yearning*, of *longing* for both an impossible external world *and* an unreachable internal world. Coleridge, Kant might say, is suffering from *Sehnsucht* aggravated by hypochondria: a yearning sickness, a longing addiction that *displaces* any present, definite object and always leaves a gap. *Sehnsucht* leaves the present with gaps, leaves the present as a gap. As Shelley succinctly puts in 'To a Skylark': 'We look before and after, / And pine for what is not' (*Works* 466). That reader of Shelley, Robert Browning, offers perhaps the best definition of *Sehnsucht* in the closing lines of 'Two in the Campagna' (1855) (*The Poems* 730):

> Just when I seemed about to learn!
> Where is the thread now? Off again!
> The old trick! Only I discern –
> Infinite passion, and the pain
> Of finite hearts that yearn.

Elusive, mercurial, always beyond one's grasp, *Sehnsucht* describes an *infinite* yearning for the *infinite*. It is a yearning *for* the infinite that remains *within* the finite world.

'He was overcome, like any booklover entering a store full of old books, with an emotion akin to a yearning, a yearning that turns into a passion all the books in the world can never satisfy', (S. Y. Agnon, *Shira* 443).

Coleridge's poem describes the structure of *Sehnsucht* in romanticism, as romanticism: a longing for *something* in the external world that only reveals a *deeper* yearning for a *hidden* internal world. One can see this in Hoffmann's *The Life and Opinions of the Tomcat Murr* (1820–1822), when Kreisler redefines Tieck's concept of *Sehnsucht*:

> Ah, no! When I felt free, I was overcome by that indescribable restlessness which so often, since my earliest youth, has made me a stranger to myself. It is not the longing [*die Sehnsucht*] which, as that profound poet so superbly said, has sprung from a higher life and lasts for ever because it is for ever unfulfilled, is neither deceived nor cheated, but merely remains unfulfilled so that it will not die; no – I often feel a wild, crazy longing [*Verlangen*] for something which I seek outside myself in restless activity, although it is hidden within me, a dark mystery, a confused, baffling dream of a paradise of the utmost contentment which even the dream cannot name, can only divine, and this idea plagues me with the torments of Tantalus. (53–4; 356)

For his part, Tomcat Murr admits: 'For some days past I had been tormented by an indescribable restlessness, an unknown marvellous yearning [*wunderbare Sehnsucht*]' (136; 451). This 'longing that can never be satisfied' is both a torment *and* a marvel (216). In *Faust* (1808), Goethe had written of 'an unbelievably sweet yearning [*Ein unbegreiflich holdes Sehnen*]' (120–1).

Coleridge's narrator is tormented, but his poem about the inability to create is also a marvellous act of creation. Without an indefinite object, without a *gap* between the external and internal world, there can be no yearning, no longing, no transcendence within the immanent world, no creation inspired by the longing to create. At the same time, Coleridge longed for this gap to be bridged, to be closed, and always sought in his Aeolian harps, his Glories, his Brocken Spectres, the spark of life to bring to life, to express, the 'shaping spirit of Imagination', and to experience an accord, a correspondence between the outer and the inner world. The Romantics are always trying to *close* the gap. When this romanticism works, it appears as an epiphany of the seamless *interchange* of the inside and the outside: Shelley on Mont Blanc: 'My own, my human mind . . . Holding an unremitting interchange / With the clear universe of things around' (*Works* 2: 37–40); Wordsworth on Snowdon discovering, 'A balance, an ennobling interchange / Of action from within and from without' (*The Prelude* XII: 508 [1805]).

As the late Roy Porter noted, the eighteenth century was a century of *les malades imaginaires* and from the seventeenth to the nineteenth century hypochondria changed from an organic disease of the chest and abdomen to a mental and nervous disorder (*Quacks* 71–4). Jane Austen's last, unfinished and untitled novel, "Sanditon", is an all too brief commentary on the culture of hypochondria in early nineteenth-century Britain. In a letter to Thomas Poole in 1803, Coleridge finds Wordsworth 'a brooder over his painful hypocondriacal Sensations' and writing again in 1804, worries that Wordsworth has become 'benetted in hypochondriacal Fancies' which 'thicken . . . his Moral Eye' (*Letters* II 1010, 1013). As for Wordsworth, writing to Poole himself about Coleridge in 1809, he concludes that 'the disease of his mind is that he perpetually looks out of himself for those obstacles to his utility which exist only in himself' (*Letters* 125–6). Coleridge's 'opium-poisoned Imagination' – as he himself described it to Byron in 1816 (*Letters* IV 628–9) – will become the "London" of Wordsworth's romanticism: a 'Babel din' of 'shifting pantomimic scenes', a 'Parliament of Monsters' 'reared upon the base of outward things' (*The Prelude* VII: 258, 266, 290).

In the 1805 *Prelude*, Wordsworth argues that in the cities 'the human heart is sick' (XII (2) 202). Sickness is 'a transport of the outward senses' (XII: 89), those mere 'vanishings,' as he calls them in 'Ode: Intimations of

Immortality' (*Selected Poems* §9: 145). But even Wordsworth acknowledges that 'the Poet . . . hath . . . His fits when he is neither sick nor well' and that he 'yearns toward some philosophic song' (*The Prelude* I: 135–7, 230). *Sehnsucht*, a *yearning* for a hidden inner world and a longing for something outside, for an 'interchange / Of action from within and from without', is perhaps the *possibility* of this romanticism. Without a prior gap, there can be no interchange. *Before* the 'shaping Imagination', *before* the responsive 'action . . . from without', there is an *indefinite* gap between the internal and external world. *Sehnsucht* is the genesis and structure of transcendence. Coleridge's 'Dejection: An Ode' can be read as the unacknowledged origin of *The Prelude*. Perhaps the poems of Colesworth or Wordsridge still remain to be read.

For Kant, a Romantic transcendence arising from a *Sehnsucht* aggravated by hypochondria would be an illness of the 'inventive imagination' that seeks to recover its lack of a definite object through . . . the inventive imagination: it is an illness without a cure. *Sehnsucht* never procrastinates, never puts off or wards off its terrible, *indefinite* longing as the source of an endlessly inventive imagination. It just opens, is opened by, a gap that it yearns to close. In *The Conflict of Faculties*, Kant himself goes on to admit that 'I myself have a natural disposition [*eine natürliche Anlage*] to hypochondria', though he puts this down not to the inventive imagination but, more traditionally, to a 'flat and narrow chest, which leaves little room for the movement of the heart and lungs' (318–19; 379). If only, as Hazlitt suggested, Coleridge had had a larger nose: 'his nose, the rudder of the face, the index of the will, was small, feeble, nothing' ('My first acquaintance with poets' 214).

Having decided that his hypochondria was 'purely mechanical' in its origins, Kant the philosopher mastered his 'oppressive' feelings by 'mental work', which 'can set another kind of heightened vital feeling against the limitations that affect the body alone'. Kant remained addicted to reason. Two months before Coleridge set sail for Malta in 1804, and always too soon, death came for that great procrastinator and self-confessed hypochondriac, Immanuel Kant.

29 November 2004. *Enter* TIME: 'I that please some, try all; both joy and terror / Of good and bad; that makes and unfolds error . . . Impute it not a crime / To me or my swift passage that I slide / O'er sixteen years and leave the growth untried / Of that wide gap, since it is in my power / To o'erthrow law' (Shakespeare, *The Winter's Tale* IV. 1: 1–8).

For Hegel, there can be a history of philosophy because thought makes its *own* outside. Through development (internal division and differentiation) and the concrete (the unification of difference into totality), the mind (*Geistes*) 'establishes itself as external to itself'. Without the need for sense-perception, it creates its own relation to 'externality [*Äußerlichkeit*]'. Time is a 'form' of externality and 'pure Philosophy appears in thought as a progressive existence in time [*in der Zeit*]' (*Lectures* 32–3; 51–2). The history of philosophy cannot be a history of the past. *In* time (as a form of externality), the history of the truth can only *be* 'beyond all time': 'as far as it is in time, it is true always and for every time'. The history of philosophy can only be a history of 'the living present [*gegenwärtig Lebendigen*]', history *as* the living present. Hegel concludes:

Such work is not only deposited in the temple of Memory [*Tempel der Erinnerung*] as forms of times gone by, but is just as present as living [*ebenso gegenwärtig, ebenso lebendig*] now as at the time of its production. The effects produced and work performed are not again destroyed or interrupted by what succeeds [*aufgehoben*], for they are such that we must ourselves be present in them. They have as medium neither canvas, paper, marble [*nicht Leinwand, noch das Papier, noch Marmor*], nor representation or memorial to preserve them. These mediums are themselves transient [*vergänglich*], or else form a basis for what is such. But they do have Thought [*Denken*], Notion [*Begriff*], and the eternal Being of Mind [*Wesen des Geistes*], which moths cannot corrupt, nor thieves break through and steal. (38–9; 58)

One cannot, one should not, *write* a history of philosophy. Plato and Hegel *write* about *not* writing history. This is where Derrida begins.

Reflecting on the French response to Hegel in the 1950s, Derrida writes in the *Specters of Marx* (1993):

Permit me to recall very briefly that a certain deconstructive procedure, at least the one in which I thought I had to engage, consisted from the outset in putting into question the onto-theo- but also archeo-teleological concept of history – in Hegel, Marx, or even in the epochal thinking of Heidegger. Not in order to oppose it with an end of history or an anhistoricity, but, on the contrary, in order to show that this onto-theo-archeo-teleology locks up [*verrouille*], neutralizes, and finally cancels historicity [*annule l'historicité*]. It was then a matter of thinking another historicity [*une autre historicité*] – not a new history or still less a "new historicism," but another opening of event-ness as historicity [*une autre ouverture de l'événementialité comme historicité*] that permitted one not to renounce, but on the contrary to open up access to an affirmative thinking of the messianic and emancipatory promise as promise: as *promise* and not as onto-theological or teleo-eschatological program or design. (74–5; 125–6)

This promise, Derrida suggests in an interview from the same year, 'is an experience that is *a priori* messianic, but *a priori* exposed, in its very anticipation, to what can only be determined *a posteriori* by the event' ('The deconstruction of actuality' 95). For Derrida, the event is *always to come* and the *promise* (the future that is not simply *of* the present) can only be indicated by a 'desolate anticipation deprived of horizon' (95). In *The Historian's Craft*, Marc Bloch had suggested that historiography is reliant on traces that are always 'witnesses in spite of themselves'. They are traces that always *exceed* the archive, that *sur-vivent* the archive, if you like. These precarious traces *of the future* constitute the traces of the past that make the writing of history possible – and the preface to an impossible mourning.

The promise of a gap that moves.

30 November 2004. There is always more than one date in the work. Writing with *dates*, gaps are unavoidable. Writing with dates: a 'putting-into-series, without model, without precedent', *14 December 1977* ('Cartouches' 223). 'Succession [*Riehe*]', Hegel argues, 'is the systematization of the science of Philosophy itself' (*Lectures* 39; 58). Succession *as* systematization: history *as* spirit. In 'Et cetera . . . (and so on, und so weiter, and so forth, et ainsi de suite, und so überall, etc.)' (2000), Derrida writes:

There is addition or seriality (and . . . and . . . and), there is supplementarity only when discrete units are hollowed out [*creusent*], in some sense, or rather indicate negatively [*en creux*] the possibility of being-alone and of being singular, of separation, of distinction, i.e., also of being-other [*l'être-autre*], and therefore of a certain disjunction, and also of an unbinding [*déliaison*], a relation without relation. (288–9; 25)

Hegel's remarkable concept for the history of philosophy – progressive succession as systematization – is always pre-ceded by gaps, by history as the history of the departures from totality. The *Aufhebung* should take care of any gaps in progressive succession as systematization. The *Aufhebung* is always a representative of 'the living present' because it retains and idealizes the best of the past for the realization and progression of the present (*Lectures* 41). However, Hegel himself *follows* this affirmation of a history of philosophy with six pages on the problem of anachronism (43–9).

Anachronism is an error – as Shakespeare writes in *The Winter's Tale*, time 'makes and unfolds error'. It is an error in computing time or fixing dates, a relating of an event, custom, or circumstance to a wrong period of time. It (is) someone or something out of harmony with time (*OED*). Anachronism (is) an error of time (*khronos*), of the wrong time, of time as an error, of time as a repetition, a return, a going back, a renewal (*ana*) that (is) out of step, that makes the wrong step (*pas*) for succession as systematization. For Derrida, anachronism (is) indicative of an unavoidable *contretemps*: time is 'out of joint', untimely ('Aphorism countertime'; *Specters of Marx*).

Anachronism '*spreads* [écarte] the present' ('Circumfession' 150; 142).

'We are too apt', Hegel warns, 'to mould the ancient philosophers into our own forms of thought, but this is just to constitute the progress of development' (44). We expect that the past can be addressed in terms of the present, but what else can one expect when there is no past and no time in the *history* of philosophy beyond the 'externality' of the mind thinking its *own* outside? Anachronism may be a problem of time, but it is also a problem of thought, of *thinking* a history of philosophy. Anachronism produces *fictions* that appear to be historical facts (43). These fictions create or expose a *gap* between succession (thought) and history (periods in time, of time). 'The sequence of thought is evident', Hegel insists, because thought is progressive development, 'but historically it is not justified' (44). A gap, a *contretemps* remains (remains to come) between thought and time.

Hegel attempts to close, to bridge, this gap by first turning back to the architecture of totality, to the part–whole relation. Each philosophy is 'of its own day', in time and of the past, and it is *also* just 'a particular stage in the development of the whole process', 'a link [*Glied*] in the whole chain [*Kette*] of spiritual development' (45; 65). He then turns from the histories of philosophy – it is the *écarts* that open up this plural – to *us*, to the listeners, readers and observers. If *we* linger too long, if we tarry too long, if we go back to the past at the expense of the present, if we get caught by time at the cost of the progress of thought, the mind will not get the same 'satisfaction [*Befriedigung*]' (45; 65).

We are only really satisfied when the mind is searching for 'the conception which already constitutes its inward determination' (46). We can only be satisfied when a *history* of philosophy is a reflection of the mind using its *own* difference to make its *own* outside to come fully and truly to its *own* inside. In the philosophy *of* the past, of a past that is privileged and separated from or taken out of the history of spirit, from the history of philosophy as 'the living present', the 'Idea is not yet present [*noch nicht vorhanden*] in its determinate character' (41, 46; 65). It is an idea that will not give us much satisfaction. It remains incomplete: a remainder, a gap in the history of philosophy.

Anachronism as *contretemps* (is) the impossible mourning of writing in the past tense, of writing in the past tense about Jacques Derrida, about the gaps that he has left behind, left *before* and *in front of him*, about writing after the death of Jacques Derrida, about that 'professor of the history of philosophy' as *Critical Inquiry* described him in 1980 ('The law of genre' 56), who spent a lifetime professing about the inescapable importance, the intolerable necessity, of the *history* of *philosophy* as the history of the departures from totality. If a history of the gaps that the life and death of Jacques Derrida has left *before us* and *in front of us* is possible, one cannot simply *place* the work of Derrida in a history of philosophy, in a history of philosophy that has *already* been written by Plato and Hegel.

For Hegel, anachronism as *contretemps* is also a problem of an untimely renewal, return and repetition, and he moves from the inevitable dissatisfaction of getting caught by the past, by a particular moment in the past, to the question of the Renaissance as the attempt to 're-waken [*wiedererwecken*]' ancient Greek philosophy (46; 65). Such a return to or repetition of the past can be seen as an 'impossibility' and a foolish attempt 'to bring back [*zurückbringen*]' the present *to* the past. The Renaissance, Hegel argues, was not simply a 'revival [*Wiederauflebung*]' of the past (a revival that takes the present to the past), but a 're-animation [*Aufwärmung*] of the old philosophies' (an *Aufhebung* of the past by the present) (46; 65–6). All 'reconstructions and repetitions [*Wiederholen (Wiederlernen)*]', all attempts to return, renew, revive the past (as the gap between thought and time) are nothing more than transitory moments that offer no true 'satisfaction'; they are 'translations only and not originals [*nur Übersetzungen, keine Originale*]', a wandering in 'a language which is dead [*erstorbenen Sprache*]', an attempt to escape the complexities of the modern world, as if one were 'to turn back to the customs and ideas of the savages of the North American forests' (47; 66).

All of this anachronism – treating the past as the present and making fictions, privileging the past over the present and losing the history of philosophy as a reflection of the developing concrete mind – all of this, Hegel says, is caused by 'the desire [the yearning, the longing, *die Sehnsucht*] for an origin [*Anfang*] and for a fixed point of departure [*Ausgangspunkt*]' (47; 67). *Sehnsucht* opens the gaps between thought and time. This desire 'must be sought for in Thought and Idea alone [*ist in dem Denken und der Idee selbst*]' (47; 67). It is only when we look for the origin and the point of departure in thought alone that we can avoid gaps in the history of philosophy. For Hegel, 'mummies when brought amongst living beings [*lebendige*] cannot there remain [*aushalten*]' (46; 66). It is only by finding the origin solely in thought that we can avoid the repetition of the past as the past (as the replacement and displacement of the living present, as the future of the past) and the translations and the dead languages and the mummies (that remain amongst the living) and the savages in the forests – and the 'canvas, paper, marble'. This is where Derrida begins, with writing.

3

The Gap Moves (1–17 December 2004)

1 December 2004. How does one avoid the monu-memorialization of Jacques Derrida? How does one write a narrative, or a story even (*un récit*), of the work of Jacques Derrida after 8–9 October 2004?

> What is the father? we asked earlier. The father is [*Le père est*]. The father is (the son lost). Writing, the lost son, does not answer this question – it writes (itself) [*(s') écrit*]: (that) the father *is not*, that is to say, is not present. When it is no longer a spoken word fallen away from the father, writing suspends the question *what is*, which is always, tautologically, the question "what is the father?" and the reply "the father is what is." At that point a flap [*une avancée*, an overhang, the fore and aft of a ship, the extension of the wing of a plane beyond its supports; an excess, that which goes in advance, goes on ahead] is produced that can no longer be thought about within the familiar opposition of father to son, speech to writing. ('Plato's pharmacy' 146; 183)

Keith Crome from Manchester Metropolitan University has very kindly sent me a copy (a copy of a copy) of the film *Derrida* (2002) (Dick and Kofman). It arrived today. I would like to see it and I am reluctant to see it. It is not so much that I am afraid of losing or contaminating the fleeting impressions I have of seeing and hearing Jacques Derrida (15 March 1991, October 1992–February 1993), but an anxiety about getting too close to Derrida (but, already, it is a question of getting too close to *Derrida* the film). I keep thinking about that passage in *Echographies of Television* (1993–1996), but I don't want to write about it because it is too obvious, too direct, too much like reading *Chaque fois unique* to say something about the death of Derrida without remembering the title: *Chaque fois unique, la fin du monde* [*Each Time Unique, The End of the World*] (a title which was first advertised in *Voyous* [*Rogues*] as: À la vie à la mort, *à paraître* – From life to death, Undying, Friends for life, For life, *to appear*). The passage – I don't want to quote it – is about Derrida watching the film *Ghostdance* and seeing the actress Pascale Ogier, who had died since the film was made, responding to Derrida's rehearsed question if she believed in ghosts, 'and she knew, just as we know, that even if she hadn't died in the interval [in the gap], one day, it would be a dead woman who said, "I am dead" ' (119–20). Perhaps it is only now that I understand the spectres that Derrida never stopped talking about, *à la vie à la mort, à paraître*.

As if I could avoid getting too close to spectres.

A digression ('it has been my plan throughout this work'). 'To write is always to rave a little.' I love this qualification: a little. To write is always to rave, *a little*. This is what St Quentin Miller, the writer, says to Anna as they discuss Portia's diary at the beginning of Elizabeth Bowen's *The Death of the Heart* (1938) (10). What does it mean to rave a little? Is this what writing always does: rave a little? To rave, the *OED* tells us, is to be mad, to show signs of madness through talking wildly, furiously, deliriously. To rave is also to be a little less than mad, to express an infatuated, laudatory or enthusiastic view about something or someone. To rave can also mean to wander, to stray, to tear, to pry, to poke. It is perhaps in this last sense that one could read St Quentin's words, 'to write is always to rave a little' because Portia's diary has somehow pried or poked or torn its way into the lives of Anna and Thomas – though it is Anna and not Portia whom St Quentin will later criticize for raving: 'You did not do well, Anna – raving about those bears' (29). 'I can neither look nor not look, only speculate, you will call it raving [*délirer*] again' (Derrida, 'Envois' 18; 22). But perhaps today, or in the last ten years, one would read 'to write is always to rave a little' as an invitation to an illicit event, to a rave? But taking ecstasy at a rave is of course merely an echo of a whole tradition of raving.

In Britain, taking ecstasy has been a problem since at least the 1650s, in the wild days of the Commonwealth, when writers such as Thomas Hobbes, Henry More and Meric Casaubon warned of the dangers of enthusiasm. In the seventeenth century and eighteenth century, enthusiasm, possession by a god, taking ecstasy, went on a journey of its own in Britain, travelling from an unambiguous association with religious fanaticism to a more complex link to both an uncontrollable religious fanaticism (Hogarth) *and* to a moderated and, apparently, always polite literary appreciation (Shaftesbury). And these two kinds of enthusiasm, of raving – if they can ever really be separated – take us 'from swerve of shore to bend of bay' back to the Muses and Socrates' daemon and creativity as *inspiration*, the work of the gods speaking through us: *that other thing than us* that creating, inventing, brings about, opens (Derrida, 'The rhetoric of drugs' 237–41; 'Psyche: Invention of the other'). Blake never stopped raving as Jesus the Imagination hovered above his bed, whispering *Jerusalem* in his ears (I: 3–5, E146). And Blanchot, in his own way, was a raver, heroically renouncing heroism: 'If to write is to surrender to the interminable, the writer who consents to sustain writing's essence loses the power to say "I" ' (*The Space of Literature* 27). Hillis Miller, a relative perhaps of St Quentin Miller, aspires to raving when he argues that the literary work is 'discovered, not fabricated' (*On Literature* 80). They are all raving, *a little*.

But what is *discovered* in *The Death of the Heart* is Portia's diary and perhaps St Quentin's observation 'that each of us keeps, battened down inside himself, a sort of lunatic giant' (310; Bennet and Royle 76–7). Raving a little we discover the raver in us: 'a sort of lunatic giant'. The transmission of this startling and disturbing discovery – and it is disturbing (there is not just a lunatic and not just a giant, but a 'sort of lunatic giant' *in us*) – is complicated and occulted enough to drive us mad. A diary is discovered that hardly says anything disturbing but disturbs everything and a writer just happens to be on hand to tell Anna who has discovered and read the diary that 'to write is always to rave a little' and all of this has been written by the writer Elizabeth Bowen and read by me and now by you, most of whom must be writers and always raving, a little. What does it mean to *write* 'to write is always to rave a little?' Four pages into the book Bowen writes this and how can anything be the same again: everything that follows is raving a little. Everything that follows is raving *a little about* raving a little. How can one read such a book? They are all raving, the writers: Portia, St Quentin, Eddie, Anna (who also writes a diary), Elizabeth Bowen. And it is three hundred pages from this announcement of a little madness to the less than reassuring conclusion that, even if we don't write, there is *in all of us* a lunatic giant. Writing, raving a little, takes us to the lunatic giant inside us.

'You were mad to ever touch the thing' (7). And it all starts with the diary, that says nothing, that only raves a little, and changes *everything*. A diary written by 'a child', who is 'more like an animal', whose writing is 'completely distorted and distorting', 'deeply hysterical' and 'not like *writing* at all' (8, 10, 11). And what is a diary? What is this kind of raving? This raving that writes *with the date*, with the incessant demand to have something to say *each day*, to write *today*, and *today* and *today* . . . 'Look how one is when it's almost always written – upstairs, late, overwrought, alone' (11). It is a writing that is always between the public and the private, not mediating but oscillating, raving a little. Not waving, drowning.

> 'If I'm to keep on writing the same way, I shall have to imagine that you do not exist.'
> '*I* don't make a difference.'
> 'You make me not alone. Being that was part of my diary.' (108)

'A writer who writes, "I am alone" ["*Je suis seul*"] . . . can be considered rather comical', Blanchot writes ('From dread to language' 3; 9). *Who* or *what* is the diarist writing to when, absurdly, she writes 'I am alone', ensuring that she is not alone? To write to oneself is always secretly, haphazardly, to address the other, to be discovered a little, *as if by chance*. ' "Oh, I wasn't looking for it", said Anna quickly' (8).

Writers keep journals to remember who they are when they are not writing, but they can only use writing, 'the very element of forgetfulness', to remember who they are (Blanchot, *The Space of Literature* 29). The writer that writes about journals, diaries, letters, about writing with a date, is always trying to remember what they can only forget. Is it a similar case even with the painter? As Lawrence Gowing has noted, the letter in Vermeer's *A Woman in Blue Reading a Letter* is illuminated, dislocated, by a light from a window that we do not see: a square of yellow, this intently studied letter looks like it is burning, like it is on fire (*Vermeer* 17–18). 'Language is overheated, words burn, and one can hardly touch them and yet one does nothing but that [*La langue est surchauffée, les mots brûlent, on peut à peine y toucher et pourtant on ne fait que cela*]' (Derrida, 'The eyes of language' 195; 476).

Raving a little one discovers . . . the lunatic giant. And what is this thing, this enthusiasm, this raving called "English Literature" or even, in Bowen's case, these two enthusiasms that can never be separated, "Anglo-Irish Literature"? 'Portia, what mean you? Wherefore rise you now?' Not Brutus's wife in *Julius Caesar* (II.1. 233), nor that giver of terrible mercy in *The Merchant of Venice* (Derrida, 'What is a "relevant" translation?'). Even though the Portia of Venice and Bowen's Portia are both narratives of 'the will of a living daughter curbed by the will of a dead father' (I. 2. 21–2).

Even though the Portia of Venice is given a letter from Antonio that has already been torn open by Bassanio, 'The paper as the body of my friend / And every word in it a gaping wound' (III. 2. 263–4).

Two hundred years before the Elizabeth Bowen Portia diary, there was the Samuel Richardson Pamela diary, *Pamela; or, Virtue Rewarded* (1740–1741), part of that epistolary madness of the first half the eighteenth century that would be superseded by the novel, by a writing without the date, a writing without the gaps of today. This epistolary madness obsessively records everything everyday, 'writing out . . . all the secrets'. '*Strange* correspondence, I call it.' A young girl starts writing and everything changes. 'This girl is always scribbling; I think she may be better employed.' 'I said, I wanted only to divert my melancholy; for I loved writing' (*Pamela* 105, 124, 54, 150). Portia carries on the tradition in *The Death of the Heart*. 'She must have bolted upstairs and written everything down' (11). 'There does not seem to be a single thing that she misses' (12). 'And you shot back and wrote it down, I suppose?' (198).

The stakes are higher for Pamela. If she doesn't write, we don't know what is happening, nothing would happen: *Virtue Rewarded*. But if Portia had not started writing, nothing would have happened: *The Death of the Heart*. Richardson's Mr B and Bowen's Anna and Eddie keep reading what is being written, to keep things going: 'He took it, without saying a word, and read it quite through.' 'As I told you, I must always see your writing.' 'I have all along showed your letters to my master.' 'I know not what I shall do! For now he will see all my private thoughts of him, and all the secrets of my heart' (*Pamela* 44, 150, 156, 263). 'And you will greatly oblige me, to shew me voluntarily what you have written. I long to see the particulars of your plot.' 'I enjoin you, Pamela, to continue your narrative' (268, 335).

'Must I recall these dates? Is it my duty to inscribe them? To whom is this due?' (Derrida, *Memoirs of the Blind* 31).

Carrying on this strange tradition, Portia is constantly questioned about her writing with the date. 'Do tell me about something. How is your diary?' (248). 'But you said you wanted my diary' (98). 'But you did say you wanted my diary' (103).

> He looked down at Portia's hand and said: 'What a fat diary!'
> Lifting her hand, she uncovered the black-backed book. 'It's more than half full', she said, 'already.'
> 'When that's done, you're going to start another?'

'Oh yes, I think so: things are always happening.'

'But suppose you stopped minding whether they did?'

'There would always be lunch and lessons and dinner. There have been days that were simply that already, but in that case I always leave a blank page.'

'Do you think they were worth a whole blank page?'

'Oh yes, because they were days, after all.'

Eddie picked the diary up and weighed it between his hands. 'And this is your thoughts, too?' he said.

'Some. But you make me wonder if I might stop thinking.'

'No, I like you to think. If you stopped, I should feel as though my watch had stopped in the night . . .' (107–8)

Pamela and Portia keep taking *time*, taking ecstasy, raving, when they write. 'He has ordered Mrs Jervis to bid me not to pass so much time in writing' (*Pamela* 58). Pamela and Portia keep writing and, somehow, they upset everything. This is what writing with the date does. Mr B reads Pamela's writing and virtue is rewarded: 'O my dear girl! You have touched me sensibly with your mournful tale' (276). Anna and Eddie read Portia's writing and the heart dies. Pamela and Portia write the narrative, they *narrate* (trying to remember what they can only forget) and like the angel Raphael in *Paradise Lost*, who tells Adam the *story* of the war in heaven and the expulsion of the rebel angels and *precipitates* the fall of man with a story, their narratives change *everything*. 'She said, in some confusion: "I do like things to happen" ' (52). 'In fact you must never write about me at all . . . just write about what happens' (108). 'It is madness to write things down' (248). 'You precipitate things. I daresay' (250). Narrative changes *everything*. It founds religions: 'This man follows me everywhere with nothing but his goatskin parchments and writes incessantly' (Bulgakov, *The Master and Margarita* 31).

And then there is something else, beyond all this writing, beyond all this raving that wanders, strays and tears. Raving a little, I hear voices. The furniture is talking ('Oh, for both of them [Heidegger and Schapiro] it's quite certain that the thing speaks . . . this thing produced by and detached from its subject begins to talk' Derrida, 'Restitutions' 323). The furniture *knows*. 'The furniture's knowing all right. Not much gets past the things in a room, I daresay, and chairs and tables don't go to the grave so soon. Every time I take the soft cloth to that stuff in the drawing-room, I could say, "Well, you know a bit more." . . . Good furniture knows what's what' (81; Bennet and Royle 78). Eric Auerbach describes this convention of *living* furniture as a kind of demonic historicism that began with

Balzac (*Mimesis* 472). And the *other* narrator of *The Death of the Heart*, Elizabeth Bowen, writes: 'After inside upheavals, it is important to fix on imperturbable *things*. Their imperturbableness . . . reminds us how exceedingly seldom the unseemly or unforeseeable raises its head' (207). Furniture *knows* that *things* are imperturbable. Imperturbable *things* somehow fend off the unforeseeable, the *things* that happen, the things precipitated by writing. This spectral furniture wards off the spectres of writing. 'Has this thing appeared again tonight?' 'I'll speak to it though hell itself should gape' (*Hamlet* I. 1. 19; I. 2. 244).

Writing *and* things: that's all there is. Things are the only alternative, the only apparent resistance to the unforeseeable: 'At Anna's, I never know what is going to happen next . . . at Anna's nothing does happen – though of course I might not know if it did' (192). Before writing makes things happen, things make things happen. Anna's apparently unintentional discovery of the diary, of the writing with the date that raves, is *prompted* by her reaction to Portia being 'so unnaturally callous about *objects*' (9). Portia writes a diary *and* she does not respect things. Matchett insists that furniture 'respects itself' (81). It is not only raving a little that leads to the death of the heart, it is also *things, objects*: 'Only in a house where one has learnt to be lonely does one have this solicitude for *things*. One's relation to them, the daily seeing or touching, begins to become love, and to lay one open to pain' (139). The things, the things that know, that remain, in truth offer no resistance to the unforeseeable. In truth they never stop talking about it: *an impossible mourning*.

For Walter Benjamin, 'the persistence which is expressed in the intention of mourning, is born of its loyalty to the word of things' (*The Origin of German Tragic Drama* 157). Writing *and* things, raving *and* mourning. The narrator in *The Search for Lost Time* returns to Paris and enters his grandmother's room unseen and, for a moment, is given 'the faculty of being suddenly the spectator of one's own absence' (*The Guermantes Way I* [II: 141]). In *Life A User's Manual* (1978), his 'biography' of the empty rooms of a Paris apartment block, Georges Perec gives an encyclopaedic account of the things in each room, inexorably marking the accumulative absence of the human occupants. 'There is not the smallest lane in Paris that doesn't say to me, literally, I hear myself whispering with each step, "I will survive you" ', Derrida writes on *2 October 1997* (*Counterpath* 102). Sorry, I'm raving a little. I'd stop, if I could.

2 December 2004. 'The double session', delivered on *26 February 1969* and *5 March 1969*, and published first in 1970 and then again in 1972 as the third part of *Dissemination*, begins with the *Philebus* and Socrates moving from *doxa* to *logos* and claiming a precedence that is (or will be, at death, after death, in the future, as the future) absolutely free of what it precedes: 'We said previously, did we not, that pleasures and pains coming from the soul alone can precede [*seule peuvent précéder*] those that come through the body? That must mean that we have anticipatory pleasures and anticipatory pains in regard to the future' (*Philebus* 39) (175; 217, trans. modified). It is the absolute precedence of the soul over the body that provides the structure for the *anticipation* of the future, for the future as a virtual presence. Kant's description of anticipation as 'all cognition through which I can cognize and determine *a priori* what belongs to empirical cognition' is not that far from Socrates (*Critique of Pure Reason* A 166/B 208). It is an anticipation to ward off spectres. Socrates illustrates this thought of anticipation, this anticipation as thought, by describing it *as* a writing and painting *of* the soul. Derrida starts 'The double session' with Socrates and with Mallarmé, and turns to 'the place of interest [*le lieu d'intérêt*]', 'this corner between [*entre*] literature and truth' (177; 219). This *third* gap in the 'splayed square [*le carré écarté*]' that makes up the four texts of *Dissemination*, supplements the question of the *history* of philosophy with the question of *literature*.

When it comes to taking an interest in the place of interest 'one cannot remain in the couple, nor in the dialectic nor in the third party' ('Istrice 2. Ick bûnn all hier' 323). The first question in this place of *dis*interest (of the interest that must be taken, *from* the impossible, and that takes me away, takes away any absolute distinction, any absolute separation, any absolute answer taken in good conscience) between (*entre*) literature and truth is '*the question of the title*', of the heading, the capital or *capitalization* of the work. Mallarmé, Derrida writes, understood the without capital, the without heading (*sans cap*), 'separating [*écartant*] the question [of the title] from itself, displacing it toward an essential indecision that leaves its very titles up in the air' (177; 220). Derrida starts with Platonic precedence and the *écarts* of Mallarmé. The 'regular intervention of the blanks [*blanc*]', 'the unfailing return, the period regularity of the white [*blanc*] in the text', the necessary, inescapable *écarts* between the printed words 'resists the authority and the presumption of the title' and 'ruins the "pious capital letter" of the title'. These *écarts blancs*, these white gaps, are 'the measure and order of dissemination, the law of spacing, the ρυθμος', the rhythm, the speeds of and as *différance* (178; 221).

Socrates moves from *doxa* to *logos*, *and* Derrida adds, to *grammata* and *zōgraphēmata*, to the 'strange relation' between the *logos*, (and the metaphors and supplements of) writing and painting (189–90). Writing and painting *illustrate*, "imitate" the interior dialogue of the soul with itself (184). Already for Hegel, this was the problem with Plato. Plato often relied on myths to illustrate, to supplement, his arguments or, as Hegel says, on 'images [*Bild*]' to illustrate 'thoughts [*Gedanken*]' (*Lectures* 87; 108). Myth is 'a superfluous adornment [*ein überflüssiger Schmuck*]' (88; 109). For Hegel, this threatens to open a gap – which should properly be 'outside Philosophy [*außerhalb der Philosophie*]' – between thought and form: 'Thought [*Gedanke*] which has itself as object [*sich selbst zum Gegenstand*], must have raised itself to its own form, to the form of thought' (*Lectures* 85, 87; 106, 108). It is 'partly the impossibility of expressing himself after the manner of pure thought [*die reine Weise des Gedankens*]' that led to Plato's reliance on mythology and 'imagery [*Bildliches*]' (87–8; 109; 'khōra' 100–2).

Hegel singles out the *Parmenides* as an example of Plato's writings where 'thought determinations [*Gedankenbestimmungen*] are used without imagery [*ohne Bildliches*]' (88; 109). Hegel may have only the imagery of myths in mind, but this seems like an extraordinary denial of the awkward opening and strange preface to the *Parmenides*. As the *Theaetetus*, which begins with a servant *reading* a dialogue between Socrates and Theaetetus *written* down by Euclid *to* Euclid and Terpsion (143), the *Parmenides* opens with the problem of the absence of Socrates, with the death of a Socrates who does not write. This absence of Socrates *invites* prefaces, narratives, writing about writing, repetition and imagery: strange suspensions of literature.

The *Parmenides* begins with a complex chain of characters all dealing with the problem of absence. For Parmenides, Zeno and Socrates to *speak*, Cephalus must *repeat* a version of the dialogue which he has heard *from* Antiphon, the original narrator, who is now *absent*. Cephalus recounts his own arrival in Athens and his meeting with Adeimantus and Glaucon. Cephalus, who appears to have *remembered* the entire dialogue between Parmenides, Zeno and Socrates, has *forgotten* the name of Antiphon, the half-brother of Adeimantus and Glaucon. It seems that Antiphon's friend Pythodorus was a friend of Zeno and that he '*remembers* a conversation which took place between Socrates, Zeno, and Parmenides *many years ago*'

(126b–c, my emphasis). Pythodorus recited the dialogue *to* Antiphon, who 'made a careful study of the piece' (126c). Antiphon has since *moved on* from philosophy to *horses* and when Cephalus *finds* his reluctant narrator, he is 'in the act of giving a bridle to a smith to be fitted' (127a). It is from this highly compressed chain of memory, repetition and absence and the *image* of the original narrator 'giving a bridle to a smith to be fitted' that the preface to the *Parmenides* comes to an end. It is always a question of form for Hegel and, as Derrida has shown, when it comes to the preface, to what pre-cedes speculative dialectics, Hegel has his own problems. 'The difficulty of representing thoughts as thoughts [*den Gedanken als Gedanken vorzustellen*]', Hegel notes, 'always attaches to the expedient of expression in sensuous form [*sinnlicher Form*]' (*Lectures* 88; 109). When you want to get on with philosophy, there is always someone who has moved on to horses.

3 December 2004. 'The imitated comes before the imitator', Derrida writes in 'The double session',

> whence the problem of time, which indeed does not fail to come up: Socrates wonders whether it would be out of the question to think that *grammata* and *zōgraphēmata* might have a relation to the future. The difficulty lies in conceiving that what is imitated could be still to come [*à venir*] with respect to what imitates, that the image can precede [*précède*] the model, that the double can come before the simple. (190; 234)

It is in this question of a Platonic precedence – *which can only pre-cede itself*, giving up its place (doubling itself) as it takes its place, as it goes before, goes in front, goes ahead (of the simple) – that 'the value of *mimēsis* is most difficult to master' (190). Derrida writes:

> Perhaps then there is always more than one [*plus qu'une seule*] *mimēsis*, and perhaps it is in the strange mirror [*l'étrange miroir*] that reflects but also displaces and distorts one *mimēsis* into the other, as though it were itself destined to mime or mask itself, that history – of literature – is lodged [*que se loge l'histoire – de la littérature –*], along with the whole of its interpretation. Everything would then be played out in the paradoxes of the supplementary double: of something that, added [*s'ajoutant*] to the simple and the one, replaces and mimes them, at once resembling and different, different because – as – resembling, the same and other than this that it doubles. (191; 235, trans. modified)

Since Plato, the 'order of *truth*' has remained that 'the double comes *after* the simple', the imitation *after* the imitated and it is 'this order of appearance, the pre-cedence [*pré-séance*] of the imitated that governs the philosophical or critical interpretations of "literature", if not the operation of literary writing' (191–2; 235–7, trans. modified).

Pre-ceding Platonic precedence: 'the history – of literature' as the history of the departures from totality, of an impossible mourning that is at once before and in front of itself.

Platonic precedence: *mimēsis* 'is always commanded by the process of truth'. Following truth, *mimēsis* is – *either* a movement of nature in which *phusis*, 'having no outside, no other, must be doubled in order to make its appearance, to appear (to itself)', *or* it is always the 'good imitation', maintaining the imitated–imitation order and remaining 'in conformity' with *phusis* (193). Between these two processes *of* truth, Derrida identifies the Platonic *gap*, the gap that Plato puts to work *for* truth, for the *history* of truth: ' "Truth" has always meant two different things, the history of the essence of truth, the truth of truth, being only the gap [*l'écart*] and the articulation between the two interpretations or processes' (192; 237, trans. modified). Platonic history is marked by the gap, but it is a gap *of* truth, the gap *as* truth, a gap in which *mimēsis* is either natural (true) or respectful of nature (true): a gap without a gap (in truth).

The 'system of *illustration*' in Mallarmé's *Mimique* diverges, swerves, deviates from the Platonic history of truth as set out in the *Philebus*. Derrida writes, 'The Mime imitates nothing [*le Mime n'imite rien*] . . . There is nothing prior to the writing of his gestures. Nothing is prescribed for him. No present has preceded [*précède*] or supervised the tracing of his writing' (194; 239). Imitating nothing, Mallarmé's text resists Platonic precedence, exposes itself to an impossible mourning. 'The Mime ought only to write himself [*s'écrire*, or even *s'écarter*, to wander, to depart from himself, to "gap" himself, as an *écart blanc*] on the white page [*blanche*] that he is' (198; 244; Bennington, 'Derrida's Mallarmé' 51, 55–6).

Mallarmé's text is 'a dramatization which *illustrates nothing*, which illustrates *the nothing* [le rien], lights up a space, re-marks a spacing as a nothing, a blank [*blanc*]' (208; 257). In the *Philebus*, Plato opens the gap between *mimēsis* and truth, to *close* the gap. He *needs* the gap to illustrate the truth. Mallarmé '*illustrates nothing*' and 're-marks . . . a blank', a gap that cannot be closed. And when the mime does not imitate, when the gaps cannot be closed, 'there remain only traces [*restent seulement des traces*] . . . which no present will have preceded or followed [*précède ni suivi*]' (211; 260). There remain only traces.

On *11 June 1977*, eight years after the double sessions were first given in Paris, one of the postcard writers in 'Envois' writes:

> He had spoken of the "*écart*" [division, interval] and today [*aujourd'hui*] I perceive – it is extraordinary that it is only today [*seulement aujourd'hui*] – that "*écart*" is the anagram of "*carte*." I had played on this inversion of the letters and of the body of words, doubtless too abundantly, for trace and écart, for *récit* [narrative] and *écrit* [writing]. And you know that if anything I abused the lexicon of the *carte*, the *cadre* [frame], the *quart* [fourth], the *cadron* [gnomon], the *cartouche*, etc. But I had never inverted *carte* into *écart*, into *écart postal*. (37; 43)

Écart traced backwards is *trace* and *trace* traced backwards is *écart*. 'Deviations [*écarts*] *without* an essential *norm*. Network of differential traces', as Derrida said in a paper at Columbia University on *6 October 1977* ('Restitutions' 269). 'The trace as gap [*la trace comme écart*]', as Derrida said in a paper at Cerisy-la-Salle on *15 July 2002* (Derrida's birthday) ('The reason of the strongest' 18). There (are) only traces, traces of what remains and of what always remains to come.

Can one ask what *is* the gap? Derrida suggests in 'The double session' that a gap "is" an *écart blanc*, a white space, blank: nothing. When one asks what *is* the gap, the *is* (*est*) always falls into the gap. As Derrida writes in 'Dissemination', the *fourth* and last gap in *Dissemination*, in Philippe Sollers' work 'the present indicative of the verb "to be" . . . is caught up [*pris*] in an operation that divided it by four. Its predominance is properly discarded [*écartée*] – that is, (s)played [*jouée*] – (drawn and) quartered [*écartelée*] by being from now on framed [*encadrée*]. From now on you will have to read the "*est*" in this *écarté* or this "*écart*" (352; 428, trans. modified). The *écarts* of *La dissémination* have at last defied the translator and become untranslatable.

'Read in the gap, it never arrives [*lu dans l'écart, il n'arrive jamais*]' ('Dissemination' 353; 429, trans. modified). The gap never arrives; the statement, the testimony even, that begins "the gap *is* . . ." never arrives. This mourning, this preface to an impossible mourning, *is* impossible. How do I begin? How do I begin when I have started with the gaps?

In 'Et cetera' (2000), Derrida argues that the 'and' (*et*) – an indispensable gap that always *invites another* gap, that insists on the plurality and seriality of gaps, the gaps of the other, as the other – cannot be reduced to the 'is' (*est*). The *et* (is) always *before* the *est*, '*before* [avant] the whole history of philosophy as ontology' (299; 31). 'Without the 'meaning' ["*sens*"] of some 'and',' Derrida writes, 'nothing would happen [*rien n'arriverait*], neither linking nor break, neither consequences nor consecution, neither conjunction nor distinction, neither connection, nor opposition, nor strategic alliance, nor juxtaposition, nor being-*with*, being-*without*, being-together, being-safe [*l'être-sauf*], not being, etc.' (299; 31). Without the gap, nothing will happen: no 'and', no white space between words, no meaning, no signification for Husserl, no critique of pure reason for Kant, no truth for Plato, no history of philosophy for Hegel. The *et* (is) always exposed to 'what happens to it, what follows or precedes it [*qui lui arrive, le suit ou le précède*]' (299; 31). 'Far from presupposing that a virgin substance thus precedes [*la précède*] or oversees it,' Derrida had written in 'The double session', 'dispersing or withholding itself in a negative second moment, dissemination *affirms* the always already divided generation of meaning' (268; 326). Gaps – never preceded by presence, always pre-ceded by the other: *contretemps, contre-espacements*.

'Signing and booking and dating, as always, *à contretemps* [*signe et livre et date, comme toujours, à contretemps*]' ('A silkworm of one's own' 344; *Voiles* 69).

5 December 2004. *A digression.* From *31 May* to *25 June 1984* Derrida gave a series of lectures in Toronto devoted to 'Language and Philosophical Institutions'. The first two lectures, under the general title 'If there is cause to translate [*S'il y a lieu de traduire*]', focus on Descartes' decision to write and to publish the *Discourse on Method* in French in 1637. A Latin translation appeared in 1644.

As Derrida remarks, in the 1640s a Latin *translation* was a rarity 'and if by chance, by deviation [*par écart*] or even a transgression, one *made the pretence* of beginning with the vulgar language [French], if one began in short with the translation, there was still cause to return [*il y avait lieu de retourner*] quickly to the supposedly normal language of origin, which should have remained Latin. The Latin version is thus nothing less than a *restitution*, a call to order or a return to order' (22; 314). The *Discourse on Method* in French was an *écart*, a deviation. In the French edition, Descartes had included a passage justifying his decision to publish in French. This passage *in* French and *on* French, Derrida notes, was deleted, erased, cleared or cleaned away (*effacé*) in the 1644 Latin translation (19, 21–2; 308–9). *S'effacer*, to erase, to wear away or wear out, also means to move aside, to withdraw, to set aside (*s'écarter*). Derrida re-traces a deviation, a gap *of* translation and a gap *in* translation: the gaps that translation relies on *and* the gaps that resist translation.

Today, I would like to trace another (dis)order of translation in Descartes. In a reversal of the history of translating the *Discourse on Method*, in 1647 a French *translation* of the *Meditations on First Philosophy* was published (the Latin text had appeared in 1641). For Derrida, these translations from the French to the Latin and from the Latin to the French mark a 'gap [*écart*] between ordinary language and a "difficult" (esoteric or formalized) language', a gap that 'can even be greater within one and the "same" language, than between two separate idioms' (24–5; 317). In the French translation of the *Meditations* from the Latin, the 'Preface to the Reader' is *replaced* by a foreword, 'The Publisher to the Reader [*Le Libraire au Lecteur*]'. In translation, the *pre-* of the preface of the author loses its proper heading to the foreword of the publisher, to the other that is at once before (in front of) and after the author's work. The Cambridge edition of Descartes' text in English has omitted this other preface. The French edition of Ferdinand Alquié has included both Descartes' preface and the foreword of the publisher of the *Meditations* in French: a doubling of the preface that would have driven Hegel to distraction.

In this excluded or double preface, 'which is probably not by Descartes', the author writes: 'One finds everywhere this version quite correct, and so respectful, that it has never deviated [*jamais elle ne s'est écartée*] from the author's meaning' (*Oeuvres Philosophiques* II: 396). *In* the gap between the Latin and the French, between the original and the translation, the foreword promises that this 'version . . . has never deviated'. The translation does not wander or swerve away from the 'author's meaning [*sens de l'auteur*]'. The foreword, 'which is probably not by Descartes', denies that there is any gap in the translation, any gap (*écart*) in the French works of Descartes. There is no *écart* in the proper name dEsCARTeS, the foreword insists. In translation, one cannot speak of gaps (*des écarts*) of the gap (*d'écart*) in the name, in the name of Descartes, of dEsCARTeS.

Despite this denial of dEsCARTeS in this double preface, Descartes had *already* written in French in the *Discourse on Method* (and later had translated into Latin) that in leaving Paris and moving to Holland he had *found* a place where, 'amidst this mass of busy people . . . I have been able to lead a life as solitary and withdrawn as if I were in the most remote desert [*j'ai pu vivre aussi solitaire et retiré que dans les déserts les plus écartés (locis maxime desertis & incultis)*]' (*Philosophical Writings* I 126; *Oeuvres Philosophiques* I: 601; *Oeuvres de Descartes* [Latin] VI: 557). Descartes creates a space, a distance, a gap between himself and Paris and finds his ideal place where the gap *works*, where the proper name works, where he can be alone *in* the crowd, '*les plus écartés*'. Les plus dEsCARTeS, Descartes is a philosopher of gaps. He *wages* everything on a gap that works: on a clean break, on a total separation, on a name that does not wander, depart, deviate or swerve, on a gap whose edges are always *clear and distinct*.

As Derrida notes in his lectures, Descartes inherited a French tradition of the gap. In the sixteenth century the French monarchy had established the laws for a 'dominant national language', a language *of* the state, founded on the principle of reducing 'the equivocation of language'. 'The value of clarity and distinctness [*La valeur de clarté et de distinction*]', Derrida writes, 'in the understanding of words, in grasping significations, will at the same time be a juridicial, administrative, policing (and therefore political) *and philosophical* value. This concern is found again in Descartes' (11; 297, trans. modified). For Derrida, if in publishing the *Discourse on Method* in French Descartes 'departs [*s'écarte*] from a certain practice and renounces a dominant usage . . . he nonetheless follows the tendency of the monarchist State, one might say that he follows the direction [*sens*] of power and reinforces the establishing of French law [*droit*]' (17; 306).

Descartes always risks in translating his works from French to Latin or from Latin to French the *écarts* of his own name, and it is for this very reason that he wages everything on a gap whose edges are always clear and distinct:

> First, I know that everything which I clearly and distinctly [*clairement et distinctement (clare & distincte)*)] understand is capable of being created by God so as to correspond exactly with my understanding of it. Hence the fact that I can clearly and distinctly understand one thing from another is enough to make me certain that the two things are distinct [*distincte ou différente (diversam)*], since they are capable of being separated [*posées séparément (seorsim poni)*], at least by God. The question of what kind of power is required to bring about such a separation [*séparation*] does not affect the judgement that the two things are distinct [*différentes (diversa)*]. Thus, simply by knowing that I exist and seeing at the same time that absolutely nothing else belongs to my nature or essence except that I am a thing, I can infer correctly that my essence consists solely in the fact that I am a thinking thing [*je suis une chose qui pense (res cogitans)*]. (*Fifth Meditation* 54; 487–8 [78, Latin edn])

But the gap travels.

6 December 2004. *A digression. We are always trying to close the gap.* In *Of Grammatology*, Derrida traces what he calls 'the economy of pity' in his reading of Rousseau. For Rousseau, *la pitié* is the most natural, most human feeling (173). [*Today*, marking again *another today*, 7 July 2005, as I am reading this I have just heard of the bomb attacks on a bus and the tubes in London.] At the same time, our pity for others must be mediated by the *imagination*. As Derrida writes, according to Rousseau, 'we neither can nor should feel the pain of others immediately and absolutely, for such an interiorization or identification would be dangerous'. The imagination 'awakens', 'arouses and limits' pity (190). It protects and preserves us from an excess of sympathy.

Our reliance on the imagination to sympathize with others also 'opens us to a certain nonpresence within presence . . . the suffering of others is [only] lived by comparison, as our nonpresent, past or future suffering' (191). We remember, we anticipate and we feel pity for others only through an image that exceeds 'sensible presence' (189). The imagination *supplements* pity. It fills a gap and, almost at once, exposes a gap that cannot be filled. The imagination, the re-presentation of pity marks 'the relationship with death' (183–7). For Rousseau, pity 'is a voice', a gentle maternal voice that preserves and protects a masculine *imperium*; writing, on the other hand, is '*without pity*' (173). Imaginative sympathy preserves and protects life, *and* it has already exposed us to the other, to death.

As Rousseau, both David Hume and Adam Smith accepted that sympathy could only be founded on the imagination (Hume, *Treatise* 319, 427). 'Our senses . . . never did, and never can, carry us beyond our own person,' Smith writes in *The Theory of Moral Sentiments* (1759–1790), 'and it is by the imagination only that we can form any conception' of the sentiments of another (9–10). For Smith, our natural sense of propriety and impropriety determines whether the passions of another person are in fact 'just and proper, and suitable to their objects' (16). If the other person is too 'loudly lamenting' or 'too much elevated' and his or her passions are deemed to be disproportionate to the situation they are in, we should not sympathize with them (22). In the six revised editions of his work, Smith would grapple with the reliability of custom, social conventions and the spectators of society to provide the grounds for a general *standard* of moral judgement and conduct. He increasingly came to rely on the imagination, at first as an ideal composite of social judgements and finally as a faculty of judgement that was entirely independent of society. We are always trying to close the gap, and every act of sympathy threatens to exceed itself. In the end, imaginative sympathy leaves us with only the imagination, which fills a gap while exposing a gaping opening that cannot be filled.

In *Art and Illusion* (1960), E. H. Gombrich suggests that imaginative sympathy is a Greek invention (115–16). In his definition of pity (*eleos*) in the *Poetics* (1453b) and the *Rhetoric* (1385b–1386b), Aristotle had already argued that when feeling the pain of another who has suffered an undeserved evil, we rely on our *own* past memories or future expectations of enduring such a pain to feel pity (Nehamas; Taplin). We remember or we anticipate our own pain and imagine the pain of the other. In *Iphigenia in Aulis*, Euripides had also already described the great *scene* of sympathy. Menelaus says to Agamemnon in Philip Vellacott's translation, 'When I see tears fall from your eyes, / My own heart melts, my tears join yours [*Ègó s' àp' ŏssou èkbalóni ìdòn dákru / ŏkteira kaùtòs àntapheká soi pálin*]' (477–8). This last phrase, *àntapheká soi pálin*, can be translated very roughly as to 'let go in turn back to you' or to 'send back to you'. Sympathy is the transference of the *tears* that transcend the gap, that melt the heart and 'touch' the 'untouchable' interiority of another. Sympathy is an involuntary, and always *natural*, letting go in turn: a sending back of tears.

'Are you going to speak to me of tears?'

'Yes, later on' (Derrida, *Memoirs of the Blind* 5).

But aren't the tears of imaginative sympathy just a kind of 'mourning for mourning', a mourning for a presence *or* absence that is, already, impossible? (Derrida, 'Ja, or the *faux-bond* II' 48).

One can contrast this Greek scene of natural sympathy with Quintillian's account of the role played by pity (*miseratio*) in the *Institutio Oratoria*. As part of the peroration, the closing statement of the defence or prosecution, 'the appeal which will carry most weight', Quintillian observes, 'is the appeal to pity, which not merely forces the judge to change his view, but even to betray his emotion by tears' (VI. 1. 23). Peroration requires the skill both to excite *and* to dispel pity (VI. 1. 46). Sympathy is not merely a natural rush of feeling, of an involuntary letting go in turn or sending back. It is a feeling that can be *directed*, that can be encouraged or impeded. The *art* of sympathy, or what Catullus calls 'false tears', is an integral part of the art of persuasion (Montaigne, 'How we weep and laugh at the same things' 263). The artifice of directing sympathy is indispensable to the *sympathia* (a relation between two terms), *consentio* (agreement) and *concordia* (correspondence) between the performer – the advocate, the actor, the writer – and his or her audience. Without the art (*tekhnē*) of sympathy, there can be no rhetoric, no judicial process, no theatre, no literature.

From the time of Euripides and Quintillian sympathy has been marked by the gap between a certain idea of human nature (and we should not forget that sympathy has long been associated with *humanitas* and as a concept of spontaneous and shared feeling it has been part of the frail fault line between the human and the animal, *Of Grammatology* 195) and the artifices and fictions of culture. *Between* nature and culture, *phusis* and *tekhnē*, sympathy raises the problem of a letting go in turn, a sending back that can never, entirely, be certain of how natural or how artificial are the sources of its shared feeling, its *tears*.

Samuel Taylor Coleridge had no doubt who the greatest practitioner of the *art* of sympathy was. In a letter from 1802, he writes:

> It is easy to cloathe Imaginary Beings with our own Thoughts & feelings; but to send ourselves out of ourselves, to *think* ourselves in to the Thoughts and Feelings of Beings in circumstances wholly & strangely different from our own: *hoc labor, hoc opus*: and who has achieved it? Perhaps only Shakespeare. (*Letters* II 810)

In *The Second Part of Henry VI* or *The First Part of the Contention of the two Famous Houses of York and Lancaster* (probably written in 1591, according to Wells and Taylor), Henry VI is possibly the *first* Shakespearian character to use the word sympathy in his *first* appearance on the stage as he praises his duplicitous wife: 'For thou hast given me in this beauteous face / A world of earthly blessings in my soul / If sympathy of love unite our thoughts' (I. 1. 23). From the start, sympathy is uncertain, conditional and, as the play will suggest, misguided. Shakespeare begins his history plays with the problem of sympathy.

It is Henry's later pity for Gloucester that hints at his inability to control his kingdom and the eventual loss of his throne and murder. Defending his time as Lord Protector, Gloucester insists, echoing Meneleus's words to Agamemnon, 'Pity was all the fault that was in me, / For I should melt at an offender's tears' (III. 1. 125–7). After he has let Gloucester be taken away, Henry says to his wife, 'Ay, Margaret, my heart is drowned with grief, / Whose flood begins to flow within mine eyes' (III. 1. 198–9). When Henry leaves, Queen Margaret remarks to Beaufort and Suffolk:

> Free lords, cold snow melts with the sun's hot beams.
> Henry my lord is cold in great affairs,
> Too full of foolish pity; and Gloucester's show
> Beguiles him as the mournful crocodile
> With sorrow snares relenting passengers. (III. 1. 223–7)

Queen Margaret argues that the tears that melt are a 'show', a dangerous artifice that have blinded and beguiled Henry. Gloucester's eyes – much like those of the last Gloucester in *King Lear* – that may or may not have melted in tears of sympathy, but which produce a beguiling sympathy in the King, have a last, terrible appearance in the play: 'But see, his face is black and full of blood; / His eyeballs further out than when he lived, / Staring full ghastly like a strangled man' (III. 2: 168–70). At the same time, a king *without* pity, like Richard III, who insists 'Tear-falling pity dwells not in this eye' (IV. 2. 67) and finds 'in myself no pity to myself' (V. 5. 157), has no more assurance of survival. The king, like the playwright, like the spectators, cannot do without sympathy and, at the same time, risks the worst – blindness, death – with too much sympathy.

It is precisely from the incalculable influence of Shakespeare that 'comedy' and 'tragedy' are defined by a blindness of sympathy (for others, from others, for oneself) that is either *almost* fatal or *always* fatal. Theatre, literature, fiction *hovers* between this almost and this always.

For Milton, as for Descartes, only God can save us from such blindness. In *Paradise Lost* (1667), 'with unexperienced thought', Eve lies down

> On the green bank, to look into the clear
> Smooth lake, that to me seemed another sky.
> As I bent down to look, just opposite
> A shape within the wat'ry gleam appeared
> Bending to look on me: I started back,
> It started back, but pleased I soon returned,
> Pleased it returned as soon with answering looks
> Of sympathy and love; there I had fixed
> Mine eyes till now, and pined with vain desire,
> Had not a voice warned me: 'What thou seest,
> What there thou seest, fair creature, is thyself.' (IV: 458–68)

In contrast to Ovid's account of the death of Narcissus (*Metamorphoses* III 442–506), which must be one of the sources of this scene, in Milton's poem God intervenes and the almost fatal blindness of auto-sympathy leads to recognition and a certain self-knowledge. But without God, we are all exposed to the danger of what Coleridge describes in *Christabel* (1797–1816) as a 'forced unconscious sympathy' for others, from others, for oneself (609).

Euripides and Shakespeare highlight the double nature of sympathy in the theatre: a particular instance of sympathy (between characters on the stage) is always telling us something about the general nature of the theatre and sympathy (between the spectators and the actors). The complexity of this 'show', which inspires and commands tears that melt, and perhaps – *for a single moment* – dissolves the barrier, blurs the distinction, loses hold of the gap between the artifice of the production and natural feelings of the spectator, would haunt Dr Johnson. Writing in the midst of the eighteenth-century confidence in imaginative sympathy as a source of sensibility, morality and social cohesion, Dr Johnson insisted in the preface to his 1765 edition of Shakespeare,

> It is false that any representation is mistaken for reality; that any dramatick fable in its materiality was ever credible, or, for a single moment, was ever credited . . . Delusion, if delusion be admitted, has no certain limitation; if the spectator can once be persuaded . . . he is in a state of elevation above the reach of reason, or of truth. (24)

One can perhaps *never* distinguish between the art and the nature of sympathy, between a directed and an involuntary sympathy. Sympathy can, to some extent, be directed (in the sense of being pointed in a direction to which it may not arrive or which it may exceed) *and* at the same time it resists all direction. Sympathy is always vulnerable to direction *and* it remains directionless. Sympathy as art, as artifice, as a kind of tool or *tekhnē* of manipulation, remains excessive, exceeding its own directions. We are always trying to close the gap *with* sympathy and can never close the gaps *of* sympathy.

7 December 2004. *A digression* (continued). The first readers of Henry James's *Daisy Miller* in 1878 were perhaps fascinated not only by the unanswered question of the heroine's innocence, but also by the strange absence of any imaginative sympathy in the story. Beneath the misunderstandings and confusions between the European and the American – 'He felt he had lived at Geneva so long as to have got morally muddled; he had lost the right sense for the young American tone' (15) – lies a far more stark absence of what George Eliot calls 'fellow-feeling'. The impossibility of knowing whether Daisy Miller is innocent or experienced, credulously or knowingly vulgar, reveals the loss of the commonly assumed and always uncertain public language of sympathy that had emerged in the age of Rousseau, Hume and Smith. Winterbourne may be 'a man of imagination and, as our ancestors used to say, of sensibility' (34), but he can never enter into the feelings of Daisy Miller: she remains opaque, 'an inscrutable combination of audacity and innocence' in both life and death (51).

Such had been Adam Smith's early confidence in the unstable power of imaginative sympathy that he argued that 'we sympathize even with the dead . . . putting ourselves in their situation, and . . . lodging, if I may be allowed to say so, our own living souls in their inanimated bodies' (*The Theory of Moral Sentiments* 12–13). Until the late nineteenth century sympathy had always been a kind of monu-memorialization, a touching of the untouchable as reanimation, redemption and resurrection.

George Eliot's novels of the 1870s reveal the anxiety about the failing powers of imaginative sympathy (Argyros; Jaffe; During). Eliot's late work is driven by the need to *restore* the place of sympathy in society, to close the gaping opening that threatens our ability *to touch the untouchable*. In *Middlemarch* (1871–1872), it is the mild enthusiast Dorothea Brooke's sense of a lack of 'sympathetic understanding' in the neighbourhood of Tipton that leads her, mistakenly, to seek it in Casaubon (28, 33). Imbued with a 'full current of sympathetic motive' in all her 'ideas and impulses', Dorothea is attracted to a man who, through his own experience of isolation, is incapable of sympathy (85–6). Lacking public sympathy, neither Dorothea nor Casaubon can find a private sympathy in marriage (49). Though Rosamond's artful sympathy is the apparent antithesis of Dorothea's natural sympathy, both women are unable to make the right judgement about the men that they marry (117). Lydgate and Rosamond are brought together by an ostensible sympathy, enjoying 'a delightful interchange of influence in their eyes', but it is a sympathy founded on a mutual ignorance of the 'inward life' and leads to a 'total missing of each other's mental track' (268, 166, 587). Eliot links this delusive external sympathy to the delusive internal sympathy that led Dorothea to marry Casaubon. It is only Fred Vincy and Mary Garth who will marry and stay in Middlemarch under the gentle, steady and habitual 'fellow-feeling' of the Garths (563–8). Caleb Garth is the ideal figure of a provincial imaginative sympathy founded on habit and custom. Garth is the David Hume of the Middlemarch of the 1820s, a world which Eliot suggests may no longer exist in the 1870s.

In contrast to Casaubon, Dorothea has an immediate sympathy with Will Ladislaw (205, 224). When sympathy works between two people it is like a 'law of nature', an immediate physical response that both expresses and exceeds (un)conscious intentions. But even when it works, sympathy remains *excessive*. For Dorothea, with neither public nor private sympathy, this natural law of sympathy can only exist as a secret, as an 'inward silent sob' (543). Dorothea and Will find a marriage of true sympathy, but only in exile from the 'provincial life' of Middlemarch.

Eliot is perhaps most conventional, most nostalgic and most explicit in her advocacy for a vanishing force of sympathy when she depicts the redemptive force of the tears of sympathy. In Chapter 81 Dorothea comes to visit Rosamond the day after she believes she has discovered an affair between Rosamond and Ladislaw. Dorothea extends her hand and 'Rosamond could not avoid meeting her glance, could not avoid putting her small hand into Dorothea's which grasped it with gentle motherliness' (793). Both Rosamond and Dorothea are involuntarily affected by the glance and *touch* of the other. Rosamond 'immediately' doubts 'her own prepossession', while Dorothea is moved to the brink of tears (795). It is a second unconscious touching of their hands that finally leads to the tears of sympathy: 'And she had unconsciously laid her hand again on the little hand that she had pressed before. Rosamond, with an overmastering pang, as if a wound within her had been probed, burst into hysterical crying' (795).

As Derrida suggests in *Le toucher, Jean-Luc Nancy* (1992–2000), there is a long philosophical and Christian tradition of touching *without* touching, of a touching that touches the untouchable, that attempts to close the most elusive, most precious of gaps. With obvious echoes in Eliot's text of doubting Thomas touching the wound of the resurrected Christ, this hapocentric scene – in which the touch of the hands signifies touching the untouchable inside of the body ('as if a wound within her had been probed') – represents the *restoration* of imaginative sympathy itself. Sympathy is saved by the gap, by the wounds of Christ.

Writing a decade after Eliot, Nietzsche rejected the emphasis on a Christian primal scene as the *last* defence of social morality. As Deleuze suggests, for Nietzsche pity is a form of bad conscience that cannot escape the guilt and vengeance of a life-denying Christian morality. Christian pathos, touching the untouchable, closing the most wondrous of gaps, is nihilism (*Nietzsche and Philosophy* 15, 36, 149–50).

One can see the influence of Nietzsche in the notable attempts in the twentieth century to *arrest* or *bypass* the Greek tradition of the tears that melt. In his call for a critical resistance (*Verfremdung*) to sympathetic identification in the theatre, Brecht argues that we must move from 'I weep when they weep, I laugh when they laugh' to 'I laugh when they weep, I weep when they laugh.' Brecht insists that in the theatre one 'must not believe that one can identify with our world by empathy' (*Brecht on Theatre* 71, 25). As Benjamin puts it in his 1939 essay on Brecht, 'instead of identifying with the characters, the audience should be educated to be astonished at the circumstances under which they function' ('What is epic theatre?' 150). Benjamin himself in 1940 extends this refusal of empathy (*Einfühlung*) to the politics of writing history. Historical materialism, he argues, has broken with

> a process of empathy whose origin is indolence of the heart, *acedia*, which despairs of grasping and holding the genuine historical image as it flares up briefly. Among medieval historians it was regarded as the root cause of sadness . . . the nature of this sadness stands out more clearly if one asks with whom the adherents of historicism actually empathize. The answer is inevitable: with the victor. ('Theses on the philosophy of history' 256)

For Brecht and Benjamin, empathy is a cultural hegemony, an aesthetic of the bourgeoisie, a depoliticization, an invitation to totalitarianism. Their emphatic refusal of the tears that melt reflects the attempt both to *overcome* the prevailing idea of sympathy as the most natural, most human of responses and to *reconstitute* the social conventions and political configurations of sympathy. While this critique of empathy is indispensable, it also assumes that the problem of sympathy as either nature *or* culture can be *resolved* and that one can *direct* or *redirect* the tears of sympathy.

Part of the reaction against sympathy in the twentieth century was also due to Husserl's insistence that empathy (*Einfühlung)* is the *possibility* of the relationship with others, of intersubjectivity (*Ideas I* §151). According to Husserl, we are 'conscious of the men on our external horizon in each case as "others": in each case "I" am conscious of them as "my" others, as those with whom I can enter into actual and potential, immediate and mediate relations of empathy' (*The Origin of Geometry* 161–2; Scheler *The Nature of Sympathy*). As Derrida points out, though *Einfühlung* does not deny the possibility of the other as *other*, it does assume an ideal transhistorical community, a society without gaps: '*Einfühlung* itself is possible only within and by virtue of the *a priori* universal structure of sociality and historicity. It supposes an immediate transcendental community of all historical civilizations and of an *Einfühlung* in general' (*Introduction* 114; *Le toucher* 216–18).

Both Heidegger and Lévinas challenged the primacy of *Einfühlung* as the origin of the relationship with the other (*Being and Time* H125; *Otherwise than Being* 125). Lévinas argues in *Totality and Infinity* (1961) that the relationship with the other that remains other cannot be reduced to 'a movement of sympathy merging us with him [*un élan de sympathie en nous confondant avec lui*]' (89; 89). Imaginative sympathy is a mode of synthesis that – despite its good intentions, despite its good conscience – colonizes and domesticates the infinite alterity of the other.

In *Le toucher* Derrida traces the readings of Husserl in France that have reconstituted the pervasive *idealization* of the tangible founded on touching the "untouchable" (the psyche, the soul). Touching – as not touching, as touching the untouchable – becomes part of 'the intuitive-continuist logic of the immediate' (148). The touch becomes an act of intuition, of plenitude and presence. As Derrida had already written in 'Dissemination', 'the pure present would be the untouched fullness [*la plénitude inentamée*], the virgin continuity of the non-cut [*non-coupure*]' (302; 367, trans. modified). It is only, Derrida argues in *Le toucher*, from 'the gap in the contact [*l'écart dans le contact*]', from the spacing that 'gives place [*donne lieu*] to *tekhnē* and the prosthetic substitute', that *contact* can be understood as 'neither fusion, not identification, nor even *immediate* contiguity' (137, 148).

Touching, Derrida had written in 'The double session', relies on a 'spacing that guarantees both the gap and the contact [*l'espacement qui assure l'écart et le contact*]' (261; 318). Some thirty years later in *Le toucher*, he returns to this question of spacing, the gap and contact. It is a matter of

an irreducible *spacing*, that is, even through what spaces the touch [*espace le toucher*], i.e. con-tact. Opening the gap [*l'écart*] in this way, giving place [*donnant lieu*] to the hiatus of non-contact at the heart of contact, this spacing makes the ordeal of non-contact the condition or the experience *itself* of contact, the *very* experience of the *same* forever open [*l'expérience* même *de contact, l'experiénce* même *du* même *à jamais ouverte*] – and spaced by the other [*par l'autre espacée*]. Such experience is affected, always, by the singularity of what, because of this spacing, takes place [*a lieu*]: therefore through the event of a coming [*l'événement d'une venue*]. *Takes place* and *takes the place of* [A lieu *et* tient lieu], I would add, to inscribe the possibility of metonymy and substitution, be it by prosthetic technique, or even the singularity of the event. (249)

It is only the gap as the *possibility* of contact that prevents touch becoming intuition. When we touch, if such a thing is possible, we touch the gap *of* the other, the gap that moves.

We are always trying to close the gap. This is what the history of imaginative sympathy tells us. We are always trying to close the gap, even when such an *absolute* closure can only end in death: 'If we had a keen vision and feeling of all ordinary human life, it would be like hearing the grass grow and the squirrel's heart beat, and we should die of that roar which lies on the other side of silence' (*Middlemarch* 194).

8 December 2004. It is two months today, sometime in the night, that Jacques Derrida died. For the first time, yesterday in Blackwell's I saw the closed parentheses and the past tense. The back of the new Continuum edition of *Positions* read: *Jacques Derrida (1930–2004) was Director of Studies at the Ecole des Hautes Etudes en Sciences Sociales.* How can one avoid making a monument of *Jacques Derrida (1930–2004)*? At the same time, the second volume of the Stanford translation of *Droit à la philosophie*, *Eyes of the University: Right to Philosophy 2* has just arrived on the shelves. On its back cover it reads: *Jacques Derrida is Director of Studies at the Ecole des Hautes Etudes en Sciences Sociales.* Two months after his death: still somewhere between 'is' and 'was', in the gap between an open parenthesis and the closed parentheses.

15 March 1991. I promised that I would write to you. The evening traffic is now racing up from the Seine along the Rue St Jacques, yellow headlights moving in the hovering blue darkness. I am writing on a small card table. I don't know how long I will stay here. Jean-Pierre, the manager of the hotel, is a misanthrope with a clubfoot and each night I hear him struggling up the stairs and calling out pas de bruit *to silence the lingering signs of life. The owners, Monsieur and Madame Renard, speak highly of the Americans who liberated Paris in 1944 and are content to make a living from offering sad little rooms to their grandchildren and to the self-imposed exiles who came to Paris in search of authenticity. Madame Renard is a kind, distracted woman in the early stages of senility and asks every morning if I have just arrived in the hotel and would like a room. They own a large and unpleasant Dalmatian, who has been trained to bite most Parisians and all Africans. The dog is an epileptic and often collapses on the floor and foams at the mouth and almost deserves sympathy, as it lies prone and whimpering after an attack. A few months ago, Monsieur and Madame Renard adopted a three-legged, incontinent cat that hobbled up and down the stairs, peeing at will. One day the cat was gone. Monsieur Renard's father, who is in his late 80s, sits all day in the reception, watching MTV. Each morning as I come to see if I have any letters he greets me with a death-rattling, never-ending* bonjouuuur. *At night, when I am coming in to go to bed he is still there and shouts out* bonsoirrrrr. *One day he was also gone. He had died in the night.*

Yesterday, I was walking on the Boulevard Saint Michel when I saw the latest Magazine littéraire *had a drawing of Derrida on the cover. I bought a copy and sat under the plane trees in the Luxembourg Gardens watching old men and women play boule, a languorous indifference masking ancient rivalries. There are some wonderful photos of Derrida and a long interview where he talks about his early life in Algeria. At the end of article, I stumbled across a small paragraph*: 'La FNAC organise une rencontre autour du livre Jacques Derrida qui paraît au Seuil. Daniel Mesguich en donnera une lecture, Jacques Derrida et Geoffrey Bennington débattront avec le public. A la Coupole, le 15 mars à 17 h 30.'

In La Coupole the beautiful people sat in gestures, as if each movement were a photograph waiting to be taken. The old guard, those of La République anci- enne, *would arrive and languidly shake hands with their few surviving comrades and ask, with infinite regret,* ca va? *It was five o'clock. I had been sitting here for nearly an hour. The launch was at five-thirty. I was looking for signs of the kind of people who would attend a Derrida launch – a launch? Like a ship, an ocean liner or, because I am reading* Moby Dick, *a whale, a Leviathan. And I read Melville*: 'It is vain to attempt a clear classification of the Leviathan . . . he eludes both hunters and philosophers' (151).

And then I saw Jacques Derrida. He appeared near the front door, stood for a moment, looked at his watch and then, like the White Rabbit, disappeared down what must have been some stairs. It was only just past five o'clock. I couldn't go down. Obviously, no one had arrived yet. What could I say, alone, with *Derrida?*

I waited ten more minutes. Finally, I stood up and walked over to the stairs and went down, expecting to find a room with Derrida sitting alone, looking at his watch. I only found the male and female toilets on my left and my right and, in front of me, a dead end: a huge mirror with my own reflection. The launch couldn't be in the toilets? And if so, which one? *How was I to respond to this sexual difference? Or was the Derrida I had seen only an apparition, a ghost? Or was it all a joke, a two-way mirror with Derrida on the other side,* tout autre- ment, *and me, in search of the philosopher, only finding a re-presentation, a reflection of myself?*

I opened the door of the men's toilets to see if there was another door and found only a bare wall. I didn't have the courage to open the door to the women's toilets.

I went back upstairs and stood aimlessly near the front door, unsure what to do, when I caught sight of a copy of Derrida's new book, Jacques Derrida, *in the pocket of a man walking on the street. He was a large, unshaven man in a heavy coat, with a short, severe haircut and a huge cigar in his mouth. He looked like a character in Fassbinder's* Berlin Alexanderplatz. *I walked out of La Coupole and followed him.*

The man walked to the end of La Coupole and went down some narrow stairs. I followed him and soon found myself standing with a large crowd waiting to enter a subterranean door. Eventually, the door opened and we entered an art deco ballroom with ornate columns, a bright metallic bar and mirrors everywhere. On a stage in front of rows of chairs sat a man and a woman. There were perhaps eighty people in the room. As I sat down, I saw Jacques Derrida warmly greeting friends and colleagues. The lights dimmed and sparse, discordant music began.

A light came up on the stage and the man, cigarette in mouth, began reading at great speed, followed by the woman reading very, very slowly. As the woman read on and on, the audience began talking amongst themselves and people began to leave, until an intermission was announced and the woman left the stage, shrugging her shoulders. When the lights faded again, the man read for perhaps half an hour without a pause. In the darkness of this underground world, I could also hear someone else talking in Latin. At some point, I realized that this third voice was a tape recording. Slides were shown with pictures of Derrida as a child and a young man in Algeria and paintings of St Augustine, who was also born in Algeria. After a small eternity, the performance ended and Jacques Derrida and Geoffrey Bennington came on to the stage.

Let me attempt to give you some fragments of the different Derridas I saw, of chaque *Jacques Derrida. At a distance, what is most striking is his brilliant white hair. Though he is sixty, he looks as if he is in his mid-forties. This Derrida could be compared to the man with the great mane of white hair sitting on the far right in Joseph Wright's remarkable painting* An Experiment on a Bird in the Air Pump *in the London National Gallery. Solitary, deep in thought, he sits somewhere between the Enlightenment experiment and the veiled moon revealed behind the curtains* (derrière les rideaux). *Another Derrida looks something like Peter Falk* (Columbo, Wings of Desire). *He has small, thick hands. His voice is surprisingly quiet. It seems modest, full of a gracious deference and humour and yet, at the same time, it has an absolute rigorous confidence, an exceptional pedagogical clarity. He uses his hands as measured tools of punctuation.*

When Jacques Derrida finishes speaking, there is applause and the lights come on. The centre of gravity, he is soon surrounded as he signs copies of his new book. . . . And then I am walking on the Boulevard Montparnasse back to my hotel, the last of the spring sun falling across the white paths of the Luxembourg Gardens. Or was I, like Cocteau's Orpheus, still standing in front of the mirror, darkly, invoking the White Rabbit, the underworld, spirits, ghosts? Je rêve . . .

9 December 2004. I have started to watch the film *Derrida* and when I saw Derrida get into his car at the beginning of the film I remembered that I did see him again, after 15 March 1991 and after the 1992–1993 seminars. In March 1994, I was walking down the Rue Soufflot with Carmella to the Luxembourg Gardens. We were talking intently and I narrowly missed walking into a car that was turning down that philosopher's road, the Rue Victor Cousin. I caught sight of the driver: it was Derrida.

10 December 2004. 'No undoing will undo the first undoing', Joyce (*Ulysses* 251). One can never simply celebrate in *good conscience* a history of *écarts*, if such a thing is possible. There are the gaps that are imposed, that cannot be chosen or ever closed: the gaps of exclusion, expulsion, exile – *and of death, most of all. Écart*: distance, departure, separation. *Écarter*: setting aside, pushing aside, removing, withdrawing, dismissing, excluding. In 1942, as a Jew, Jacques Derrida was *expelled, excluded, dismissed* from his school in Algeria by the French authorities – '*renvoyé*', he writes in *La carte postale* (97), '*chassé*', '*expulsé*' in 'Circonfession' (57, 266). In 'Abraham, l'autre' (2000), he describes this event of anti-semitism as 'a caesura that seems to determine itself, to cut itself out of the wound itself, the wound that cannot be healed [*se découper dans la blessure même, dans la blessure non cicatrisable*]' (24).

Derrida cites and recites this event in *The Post Card*, 'Circumfession', *Monolingualism of the Other* and 'Abraham, l'autre', until it becomes a kind of story, a *récit* even. Often reluctantly, he returns, is returned, again and again to this event in interviews ('Unsealing ("the old new language")', 'A testimony given . . .', *For What Tomorrow* and *Sur parole*). Safaa Fathy has even given an account of returing with Derrida to the school that expelled him in 1942 (*Tourner les mots* 44–6). Speaking in an interview on *13 September 1991* Derrida says, 'I shouldn't place so much empahasis on this episode in my life – perhaps I already have a bit too much' ('A testimony given . . .' 55). He begins a 2002 interview by highlighting the inevitable demand for repetition in the many interviews that he has given. From the start, the singular event, *the only once*, is repeated, cited and re-cited – and exposed to the other (*Au-delà des apparences* 17).

Cited and re-cited, the event becomes *un récit*, an untranslatable word for Derrida that hovers somewhere between a narrative, a story, an account. A *récit* is neither a novel (*un roman*), nor a story (*une histoire*), nor simply a memoir (*un mémoire*), a biography or autobiography. It is somewhere in between.

> If I had to retire to an island, it would be particularly history books, memoirs, that I would doubtless take with me, and that I would read in my own way, perhaps to make literature out of them, unless it would be the other way round. ('Passions' 27–8)

How can an event *become* a kind of story, a narrative, a *récit* even? In 'La littérature au secret: Une filiation impossible' (1999), Derrida describes 'becoming-literary [*devenir-littéraire*]' as what happens when a text

> is entrusted to the public space, and relatively readable or intelligible, but whose content, meaning, referent, signature and addressee [*le destinataire*] are not clearly determinable *realities* [réalités], realities at once *non-fictitious* or *purified of all fiction* [non-fictive *ou* pures de toute fiction], realities delivered, as such, by an intuition, to some determinate judgement. (173–5)

For Derrida, 'the history – of literature [*l'histoire – de la littérature*]', as he called it in *Dissemination*, is a series of very singular and strange suspensions. These suspensions (from 'content, meaning, referent, signature and addressee') are always contingent, never absolute and inseparable from questions of democracy (the right to say everything and the right to say nothing), and a necessary, but always risky, irresponsibility at the heart of responsibility ('This strange institution called literature' 36–48; *Demeure*). A singular and cited and recited event becomes literary, becomes a story (*une histoire*), *un récit* even, when it can no longer simply be *reduced* to pure non-fiction, if such a thing were possible.

But what happens when the cited and recited event is offered as *my* story?

> That is a rather abstract way to narrate a story [*de raconter une histoire*], this fable you jealously call your story [*ton histoire*], a story which would be solely yours. (*Monolingualism* 28; 53)

If there is a story (*une histoire*) of autobiography, it is a kind of writing that always falls short of a sovereign identity. In *Monolingualism of the Other* (1991–1996), Derrida writes:

In its common concept, autobiographical anamnesis presupposes *identification*. And precisely not identity. No, an identity is never given, received, or attained; only the interminable and indefinitely phantasmatic process of identification endures. Whatever the story [*l'histoire*] of a return to oneself or to *one's home* [chez soi], into the "hut" [*"case"*] of one's home (*chez* is the *casa*), no matter what an odyssey or *Bildungsroman* it might be, in whatever manner one invents the story of a construction of the *self*, the *autos*, or the *ipse*, it is always *imagined* [*on se figure*] that one who writes should know how to say *I*. At any rate, the *identificatory modality* must have and henceforth be assured: assured of language and in its language. (28; 53)

Without the impossible assurance of identity, there are only the ruins of an auto*écart*graphy. There is always more than one gap and for Derrida in telling his story, the 'nonlocatable experience of language' which preceded the *autos* 'was neither monolingual, nor bilingual, nor plurilingual. It was neither one, nor two, nor two + n' (29). As with *Dissemination*, it is always a question of three or more gaps to mark the *Unheimlichkeit* 'of an uncountable language' (29).

Stefan Zweig's autobiography, *The World of Yesterday*, was published in 1943, the year after Derrida was expelled from his school in Algeria. Zweig describes the Vienna before the First World War as a city of cosmopolitan harmony, a Kantian utopia, a city 'which hospitably took up everything foreign' and emanated a unique 'spiritual supernationality' to the rest of Europe (13–14, 24; Derrida 'On cosmopolitanism'). After 1933, Zweig went from being one of the best-selling European authors writing in German, to an unpublishable fugitive and exile. 'Today,' he writes, 'as a writer I am, in Grillparzer's words, one "who living follows his own corpse" ' (317). In his preface, which should have been his first or last words, Zweig concludes, 'for truly I have been detached, as rarely as anyone has in the past, from all roots and from the every earth which nurtures them . . . Europe, the homeland of my heart's choice, is lost to me' (xviii). Zweig was a cosmopolitan who believed that he only spoke *one* language and that this language was *his* – the language of Europe (Derrida, *Monolingualism*).

Zweig did not survive 1942. *The World of Yesterday* ends with a publisher's postface and the reproduction of Zweig's suicide note dated *22 February 1942*. Written the day before he and his wife took their lives, Zweig writes of 'the world of my own language having disappeared for me' (437). Having lost *his* language, his only language, he was unable to go on living. According to Gershom Scholem, one can contrast Zweig to

Freud, Kafka and Benjamin, because 'they knew that they were German writers – but not Germans. . . . [and] closely as they knew themselves tied to the German language and its intellectual world, they never succumbed to the illusion of being home' ('Walter Benjamin' 190–1).

> One day I will write a long narrative [*un long récit*] for you, not a detail will be missing, not a candle light, not a flavour, not an orange, a long narrative [*un long récit*] about what the Purim cakes were in El-Biar, when I was ten years old and already understood nothing. ('Envois' 73; 81)

What happens when the singular – and always repeatable – event becomes a *récit*? In *Parages* (1976–2003), a text with a twenty-seven-year history, Derrida returns again and again to 'the force and the desire to repeat, to cite and recite' in reading the works of Blanchot ('Pas' 20). Somewhere between non-fiction and pure fiction, shuttling back and forth, neither near nor far, oscillating not drowning, the *récit* is always a kind of *narrative*, an impossible narrative *of* the strange suspensions of literature.

From the start, 'the récit always recites [*le récité récite toujours*]' ('Pas' 27). It begins *without* a present event. The repetition of the *ré-cit* marks at once a double affirmation and an impossible mourning. As an affirmation of repetition, the *ré-cit* marks a *yes, yes* that exceeds the affirmation of a present subject or object. It is an affirmation – a re-citation – that is *open* to what remains to come, *à venir*. The *ré-cit* marks the *event* as that which always *remains – to come*. The *ré-cit* also marks '*le malheur sans mesure*', a disproportion that refuses any synthesis or reconciliation, a *gaping opening* 'that will never be closed' ('Pas' 21–3; 'LIVING ON' 85–6, 104). The event *remains* – without presence, without closure – wonderfully and terribly before us *and* in front of us.

The *récit* is always returning to the relation between literature and death, *sur-vivre* if you like ('LIVING ON' 136). The amazing, strange suspensions of death in literature –

> Whitman in 'Crossing Brooklyn Ferry' calling in the past tense to his future readers, 'Just as you feel when you look on the river and sky, so I felt' (148)

> Fitzgerald in *The Great Gatsby* leading us to the death that has not arrived, 'So we drove on toward death through the cooling twilight' (129)

> García Márquez beginning *One Hundred Years of Solitude* with a death sentence

that is deferred for two hundred pages, 'Many years later, as he faced the firing squad, Colonel Aurelio Buenida was to remember that distant afternoon when his father took him to discover ice' (1)

– are perhaps not only, as Benjamin said of Kafka's stories, an instance of 'narrative art' regaining 'the significance it had in the mouth of Scheherazade: to postpone the future' ('Franz Kafka' 129). The suspensions of death in literature, the 'narrative art', the *récit* that always starts with the 'strange "pas" of *é-loignement*' ('Pas' 28, 31) and refuses any assured moment of proximity, of propriety or presence, does not only 'postpone the future', it also re-cites without rest the *future* of the past, the *finitude* of a gap that moves.

This is what "literature" and the study of literature (which is so often working with the dead) does: as soon as I repeat a story or a narrative, as soon as I cite and recite, as soon as I encounter the elusive resistance of the idiom, the part becomes greater than the whole and the *future* of the past becomes ungovernable, unbridgeable, unfillable, inventive and the boundaries of the so-called "work of mourning" – the idealization and interiorization of the dead by the living – become untenable, unworkable and mourning becomes impossible, interminable, without rest.

I keep having dreams about Derrida.

12 December 2004.   Since 12 October 2004 I have been trying to avoid the *récit* on *sur-vivre*, the great theme of *Parages*, trying to avoid Derrida's "last words" on this word from the interview in *Le Monde* on *19 August 2004*. As if I could avoid *sur-vivre*:

> I have always been interested in this thematic of surviving [*la survie*], whose meaning does *not add itself* to living or dying. It is originary: life *is* surviving [*la vie* est *survie*]. Survival in its current sense means to continue to live, but also to live *after* death . . .

> At the moment when I leave (publish) "my" book (no one forces me to), I become, appearing-disappearing, as this ineducable spectre who will have never learned to live. The trace that I leave signifies to me at once my death, to come or already come [*à venir ou déjà advenue*], and the hope that it will survive me. This is not an ambition of immortality, it is structural. I leave [*je laisse*] a bit of paper, I go, I die [*je pars, je meurs*]: it is impossible to get out of [*sortir*] this structure, it is the constant form of my life . . .

> Everything that I say – since at least 'Pas' (in *Parages*) – on surviving as the

complication of the life–death opposition proceeds for me from an uncondi-
tional affirmation of life. Survival [*la survivance*], this life beyond life, the life
more than life, and the discourse that I give is not deadly [*mortifère*], on the
contrary, it is the affirmation of a living which prefers to live and to survive
death, because surviving is not simply this which remains [*reste*], it is the most
intense possible life. ('Je suis en guerre contre moi-même' 12–13)

Today, a story, un récit even, from 1942. 'In a grievance like this, one takes
on lastingly [*à demeure*] a mourning for what one never had' (*Monolingualism* 33; 61). 'It turns out that something that never was and never will be
is all that we have' (Amos Oz, *The Same Sea* 152). 'When I was little, my
ambition was to grow up to be a book. Not a writer. People can be killed
like ants' (Amos Oz, *A Tale of Love and Darkness* 22). 'We all have so many
first names. But you also will like her name as a young orphan, I would
like to make you wait before telling you it and leaving you with it, withdrawing [*retirer*] while leaving you with it, it lacks nothing: Hadassah'
('Envois' 74; 82).

*Hadassah was small for her age, too thin to be healthy and too young to be without
illusions. Stripped of almost everything else, she had come to believe in the power of
her eye to see through the motives, the pretences and the lies of others. There had
been too much belief, too much faith in others. Watching from her medieval perch
through lead-lined glass she could see the innocents strolling on the street, oblivi-
ous, unmindful, untroubled. They could not conceive of what she took for granted:
murder in broad daylight, horror in the middle of a mundane day, the end of a
life being no more than the breaking of a stick. She could see by the way the
students walk in England that they knew nothing: sauntering along the street,
bounding with unconcern on the pavements. In Europe people walk huddled
inside themselves, hidden in their coats; only Nazis bound. When life or death has
almost nothing to do any more with the will to live, it is hard to walk down the
street, to stay alive. The walls of the college are thick, its shelves laden with books,
its rituals and traditions as arcane and exclusive as ever, but for Hadassah it is not
enough.*

*   *

*It is a farce that I see my father playing everyday. The English do not know
what to do with foreigners. Even here, where scholarship is a cosmopolitan who
speaks four languages, these strange people do not know what to do with
strangers. They all look as if they would like to burst out of their suits, but know*

they never will. Receding into themselves every time they meet someone, they are like two tortoises that have withdrawn their heads. Everything is so clipped, so minimal, so refined. And they give my father nothing but respect: no affection, no friendship, no solidarity, only respect. And they are killing him with their respect. As for me, they are killing me with their vanishing sympathy, their small, already retracting signals of fellow feeling. At the moment I venture out and peep above the parapet they have already withdrawn: they are standing in front of me and they have already gone. They are a people who are not there when they are there; magicians the lot of them. Then again I have only seen this college, this famous Oxford. But even the lower class of people, the scouts who clean the rooms and the porters at the lodge, even they have a strange joviality about them, a contrived simplicity that only tells me that they too are not there when they are there in front of you. With the power of my eye, I can see they are all actors. At home, there were no actors. There were masters, slaves and murderers.

Perhaps the English are just shy. But it is not easy to tell the difference between the shy, the shallow and the cold. I am always cold in this room, in this country, with these people, even when the sun is out. Mother had to stay and we are waiting to hear from her, but we will never hear from her. My English is getting better and if anyone is still alive when this war ends, I shall make my living as a translator. If the Nazis win, everyone will speak German and there will be no translators. If they win, my father and I will be brushed away like dust. We were blown here like dust. We are already dust.

An English boy was introduced to me yesterday. His eyes were green, green and sad. He had only just learned that his mother had died in the bombing in London. I shook his hand, as they do here; a quick shake, hardly touching the outstretched hand. I said nothing. Why should I say anything? They wanted me to make it better for him! I said nothing and I did him a favour. Perhaps I should have slapped him in the face. But if the English became hysterical all these medieval walls would fall down. They gave me this absurd book to read about one beautiful woman coming to Oxford and all the men, every single one of them, drowned themselves when they found that she could not love them. It is an irresponsible book, a book written by a man who knows nothing about war. And they gave me this to make me feel better!

Do the English dance? Do these young men have any suppleness? It seems the supple ones only like other men. It must be hard to be an Englishwoman. The women I see on the road look like either scarecrows or horses and there are more horses than scarecrows. If I live, I suppose I will have to marry one of these young men who do not dance, coaxing him into life as best I can. It will be like living with *a highly educated corpse. I now pronounce you corpse and dust. Will there be no one to inscribe me in the book of life?*

They ask me, 'How are you?' worried that I will say something. I can see the wrinkle of anxiety, the hint of more than the loss of a soldier at the front, of a bomb dropped on a house, a ship sinking in the North Atlantic, of something more than they can understand on this island. My father says it is three hundred years since the English had to fight in their own country and this is why they will win this war. Not even their great-grandparents can remember what I might say when they ask me 'How are you?' 'I am very well, thank you,' is all that I can say and all that they can hear.

I have decided to write a story.

Count Epstein owed his title to Napoleon, but everything else to his bad luck. It was only by chance that he had stepped out of the summer rain into Monsieur Renard's small bookshop on the Rue de Rennes. Monsieur Renard, who had worked his way up from the stalls on the Quai, greeted his distinguished visitor. Casting his eye across the works of Restif de la Bretonne, Madame de Staël and Madame de Charrière, Count Epstein had seen a little book by a Russian author translated into French. Feeling obliged to pay for his shelter from the rain, he bought the book. Strolling over to the Luxembourg Gardens he sat in the shade beneath a vast plane tree and cutting each page with infinite care and devotion, he began to read of the immeasurable catastrophes that formed the history of Russia. Soon the light began to fade in the gardens, the bright chalk on the paths turning first grey and then blue. As he walked aimlessly down the busy Boulevard Saint Michel, Count Epstein sat down in a café, his mind full of vast fields and toiling peasants, Cossacks, Tsars and a thousand years of cruelty and hardship. Hardly aware of what he was doing, he bought a paper and read that the French would soon be at war with Russia. Troops were to be sent to the Crimea. Though in fact the papers had written of nothing else for weeks, to Count Epstein the coincidence of the book he had found and the news of war with Russia seemed so extraordinary and he was quite overwhelmed. Haunted by the thought that he and his family owed their good fortune to Napoleon's enlightened reforms, the same Napoleon that had led the last terrible war against the Russians, and deeply moved by the suffering of the Russian people, Count Epstein decided to go to the Crimea. Driven by a compassion for the enemy and a deep sadness for the violence of men, Count Epstein found himself part of the French cavalry. Unable to kill, it was inevitable that he would be killed. Unknown to either of them, in a minor and bloody skirmish in Silistria, Count Epstein died at the hands of a young Russian officer named Lev Nikolayevich Tolstoy.

In 1854 Jacob, the eldest son of Count Epstein, inherited his father's title while managing to avoid his bad luck. He had admired his father and mourned his vulnerability to the fate of humanity and sensitivity to chance and coincidence. If a remarkable coincidence of events presented themselves to him he would only have to say the word *Cri . . . mea* under his breath to make certain that he took no notice. Count Epstein had already taken an interest in the family business, which had developed since the 1790s from craftsmanship to manufacturing, and made it a principle to avoid all signs, all intimations, of good or bad fortune. He was a man who never looked to the stars for guidance. He kept his head down and avoided the whirling chaos. He married a second cousin and brought two manufacturing families together and tended to his family as one would a vegetable garden: not too much water, not too little. He steered the family business through the Franco-Prussian war and the 1870 Commune and died somewhat before his time in 1874, almost twenty years to the day after his father. It was only after his death that his journals were found and it became apparent that he was quite mad. The twenty cloth-bound volumes, one for each year of his life as Count Epstein, were covered in a script so small that it could only be read with a magnifying glass.

The third Count Epstein, Count Philippe d'Epstein-Latour as he became known, was fourteen years old when his father died. Like the rest of the family he read his father's journals with fascination and horror. Each day of the fourteen years of his life, when he had seen his father preside over a meal or escort the family to the Bois or sit reading *The Times* with a cup of bitter chocolate, his father's journal recorded the private torment and delusions of a madman.

'It is only a novel,' his mother Sophie insisted. 'Your father thought that he was Balzac.'

Philippe was not convinced. Studying the entry for 12 November 1872, a day that he distinctly remembered, as it was his twelfth birthday, he read the following account in his father's impossibly small handwriting:

12 November 1872
There was a glorious nothing today until there was something; that terrible something crawled into the morning, broke its way into my lungs and made

me breathe. But I know that it is not my breath. It tastes of Amaretto and I have never had Amaretto in my whole life. Garibaldi has stolen everything. Who has put these teeth in my mouth? There are too many. I tried to pull the front one out, but it told me that I was a toothless beggar sitting at the gates of Jerusalem and might be the Messiah. At breakfast the hair on my head began moving to the left and all I had wanted was to sit quietly. Cri cri me a, cry for me Crimea. By lunchtime I had a tonsure. By evening I was Charles Darwin and naturally selected, natürlich, to be. But you have all misunderstood me. There was a glorious nothing today and I never asked to be.

'It is obvious that he had syphilis,' Philippe's elder sister Rachel said to him. But Philippe had noticed the recurring reference in the journals to the Crimea and came to the opinion that his father had been driven mad through the inhuman effort of avoiding all chance and coincidence in his life. Already warned by the example of his grandfather, Philippe understood that there was no alternative: he could neither give way to chance and coincidence, nor could he avoid chance and coincidence. A random life killed you and a secure life drove you mad. Philippe was only fourteen and there was really not much he could do with this imponderable dilemma, except to decide that he wanted to live.

*

If I don't become a translator, I will become a librarian. One could do worse than live with books, spending one's days putting things back into order again in a world that is ordered from the start. Imagine a library without order. Impossible. Books would jump from their rows, from their shelves, landing upside down, falling open, pages blowing in the wind from a hole in the wall, from a roof that is open to the sky and the rain would fall on the books. I have seen such a library. My father says that most of the books in the Bodleian are underground. I could work in such a library. But now, I am living in the air, in a turret with narrow winding stairs and when the bombs come there will not be time to run down; the stones in these walls are too old and too heavy.

They have given me a copy of Alice in Wonderland *and made much of the fact that the author taught at one of the colleges. Are they trying to tell me something with this mad book? Are they trying to say, we may be polite, we may be reserved, we may be desiccated human beings shrinking from life, glorying in footnotes, big heads without bodies, almost dead in fact, but in truth we talk to white rabbits and are quite mad. With the power of my eye I can see now that all these fellows are just holding on to a façade, a protocol of reason. They know that they are all mad, that all of this is a kind of madness. This is not a university: it is a sanatorium. What I have learnt from this book is that in Oxford not only books go underground. With the power of my eye I shall find the rabbit hole and when the bombs come, I shall grab my father and know where to run. And we shall live on rabbit stew.*

These women, these wives have bustled about me like missionaries in their own home. Their ignorance is astounding. It must take such willpower to be provincial in all things, to stay out of the sun and live an alabaster life. Nothing is said, but I seem to be a little Pharisee in need of an inner world. Less law and more love *their cups of tea and paste sandwiches cry out.* Less death *my gracious silence murmurs in the darkness of a fully lit room.*

Where is your mother? They ask me this and I have to stop myself saying, and where is your mother, have you also lost her, mislaid her on a garden path, in a field of buttercups? My little brother, I reply, was ill and mother stayed with him. We are waiting for them. We had a postcard a few weeks after we arrived. All that has arrived in this country of my mother is a postcard. Here we are, in this turret, above this lane, across from these sandstone walls in Oxford, and here there is only her ink, her few lines and a stamp.

My father has become unwell. He lies in bed correcting and recorrecting the proofs to an article in English that will be published in I o wa, I da ho or O hi o. It will be his first publication in America and, though neither of us have said anything, we both know that this printing of his words, his name, this first appearance on paper in the United States, is a small suitcase sent on ahead, just in case. Is there a University of Hollywood? To get a doctorate there you have to sing a bit, dance a bit, act a lot and be very good looking. I would like to go, but only to sit at the family table with Lionel Barrymore at the end of You Can't Take It With You, *or next to Jean Arthur when she plays the piano in* Only Angels Have Wings. *I would only go to America to sit in a movie.*

A friend of a friend of a friend of a colleague of my father, in other words a complete stranger, came to visit. He was dishevelled and smelt of beer, which made him seem very English. He looked like a man who would never wash again. He sat by the window and even in his heavy tweed jacket he appeared transparent in the sunlight. He held his cup of tea in both hands, his head tilted to the left and told us that everyone in the East is dead. And then I sat by the window and I saw with the power of my eye all the empty houses and all the animals, all the cats, dogs and birds that had been left alone in the empty houses, waiting.

Here we are, and my father is looking more and more like an old book on a library shelf. Here we are, and there is no going back and no going forward. In this sanatorium the greatest kindness is that there is no time and no place:

there are only books. There are only books and the doctors and patients who, with infinite care and reverence, watch over them so that they will last, so that something will survive.

13 December 2004.   *La dissémination s'écarte* – diverges, deviates, departs, parts – prefaces to *Glas*, preface to an impossible mourning for Jacques Derrida. In 'The double session', Derrida writes of 'the *interval* of the *entre*', the 'interval *between*', of the hymen and the gap (212). The hymen, 'the confusion between the present and the non-present', is 'an operation that "at once" sows confusion *between* [entre] opposites and stands *between* [entre] opposites' (212; 261, trans. modified). With the hymen, 'what takes place is only the *entre*' (214). The *gap*, the 'interval *between*', is the *possibility* of the between, of 'the in-between-ness of the hymen [*l'entre-deux de l'hymen*]', of the unavoidable 'confusion between the present and the non-present' (220, 212; 272, 261). The '*entre* of the hymen' marks 'a masked gap [*écart masquer*]' 'where nothing has yet taken place' – a gap that 'remains in the other [*reste dans l'autre*]', that remains neither present nor absent (215; 265).

The possibility of the '*entre* of the hymen' indicates a gap that does not work for Hegelianism. Derrida writes: 'At the edge of being [*au bord de l'être*], the medium of the hymen never becomes a mere mediation or work of the negative [*travail du négatif*]; it undoes [*déjoue*] all ontologies, all philosophemes, all dialectics of all borders [*tous les bords*]' (215; 265, trans. modified). The edges, the borders of the gap *move*, folding and refolding, and resist the order – the opening and closing, the inside and the outside – of the *Aufhebung*. The *rhythm* of the gap marks 'pauses and cadence, spacing and shortness of breath [*la pause et la cadence, l'espacement et l'essoufflement*]' (216; 266). The gap *moves* and casts aside being. 'The *casting aside* of "being" [*la mise à l'écart de l'"être"*] defines itself and literally (im)prints itself in dissemination, as dissemination' (216; 266).

The gap moves.

In the second session of 'The double session', it is all about *a gap that moves*.

A gap that moves, a gaping in Mallarmé's work, a gaping that cannot 'close upon itself [*se fermer sur soi*]', a gaping that marks 'the breaking through [*l'effraction*] of theatre into the book, of spacing [*l'espacement*] into interiority', a gaping that is always 'parted from itself [*lui-même écarté*]' (234; 286–7).

A gap that moves, that *speeds*: 'It dislocates all oppositions. It carries them off [*entraîne*] in a movement, impresses upon them a play that propagates itself through all the text's parts [*pièces*], constantly shifting [*déportant*] them, more or less regularly, setting them out of phase [*avec des décalages*], through unequal displacements, abrupt slowdowns or bursts of speed [*des retards ou des accélérations brusques*], strategic effects of insistence or ellipsis, but always inexorably' (236; 288–9, trans. modified).

A gap that moves, suspends, floats, *dances*: 'In folding back [*repliant*] upon itself, the text thus *parts* (with) reference [*le text écarte ainsi la référence*], spreads it like a V, a gap [*écart*] that pivots on its point, a dancer, flower, or Idea' (239; 293). A gap that dances: a 'pirouette' 'in the blank space of the inter-text' (241). 'We have recognized in the common element of these writings the rule under the name of *cast-aside-reference, being aside* [de référence écartée, être à l'écart], or hymen' (242; 296, trans. modified). Casting aside, setting aside being in the history of philosophy, in literature, in life *and* death: 'the gap, or the setting aside, of being [*l'écart de l'être*]' (242; 296).

A gap that moves in the rhythm and the strange suspensions of literature, *as* literature: 'Literature is at once reassured and threatened by the fact of depending only on its self, standing in the air, all alone, aside from being [*à l'écart de l'être*]' (281; 340). Gaps that dance: wandering, digressing, swerving, stepping aside from ontology.

Gaps dance.

Gaps dance: this is what the *four écarts* of *La dissémination* (1968–1972) affirm as a preface to *Glas* (1968–1974), as a preface to the unavoidable gaps in a 'work of mourning' that never stops mourning for its *inability* to mourn for itself *as itself*:

> To play with the four seasons [*Jouer avec le quatre des saisons*]: this play, this evil of *Sa* [*savoir absolu* – absolute knowledge], opens this play with a gap [*l'ouvre d'un écart*] that no longer assures it of being able to reappropriate itself in the trinitarian circle. This season disorder [*mal de saison*] neither destroys nor paralyses absolutely the infinite concept. If it formed only the negative of this concept, it would yet confirm that concept dialectically. Rather, it puts that concept out of order [*le détraque*], stops it, jams it [*l'enraye, le grippe*] inconceivably. Also scratches it [*le griffe*] with writing. (*Glas* 233a; 260a)

14 December 2004. The gap moves and we are always trying to close the gap, and with God most of all. 'The hidden god is apostrophized',

Derrida says in a paper from April 2003, 'he is called by his name, but called at the very moment when this performative appeal describes, states, defines the absence, withdrawal, separation, the inaccessible secret that forbids us to the very essence of God, thus the form of his substantial presence' ('Justices' 709). Derrida suggests that the hiding or withdrawal (*écarter*) of God remains within onto-theology: it announces a gap, a space, a distance that *maintains* the essence (presence *or* absence) of God: 'here the essence is called absence' (709, 719, 721). At the same time, as Heidegger implies in *Identity and Difference*, the unity of onto-theo-logy is 'determined by what differs in the difference' and the 'origin of the difference can no longer be thought of within the scope of metaphyics' (70–1). The "origin" of the absence *or* the presence of God is a difference that is *neither* absence *nor* presence. *différance*, without possible capitalization, Derrida will argue, '(is) (itself) other than absence and presence [*la différance (est) (elle-même) autre que l'absence et la présence*]' ('Différance' 23; 24).

One must always be vigilant when it comes to the proclamation of a gap, and with *the* gap (the absence) *of* or *as* God most of all. It is a question of a gap that invariably reconfirms a world without gaps, an onto-theology. As Derrida remarks in 'Signature event context' (1971):

> A written sign is proffered in the absence of the addressee [*destinataire*]. How is this absence to be qualified? One might say that the moment when I write, the addressee may be absent from my field of present perception. But is not this absence only a presence that is distant, delayed [*retardée*], or, in one form or another, idealized in its representation? It does not seem so, or at very least this distance, division [*cet écart*], delay, *différance* must be capable of being brought to a certain absolute degree of absence [*un certain absolu de l'absence*] for the structure of writing, supposing that writing exists, to be constituted. It is here that *différance* as writing could no longer (be) an (ontological) modification of presence. (315; 374–5)

A digression. At the end of *Deuteronomy* 31:16–18 God warns Moses that the Israelites 'will abandon me' and, that in turn, 'I will abandon them and I will conceal my face from them; (they) will be (ripe) for devouring . . . I will conceal, yes, conceal my face on that day' (*The Five Books of Moses*, Fox trans.). God will, at some future point, *react* to the actions of Israelites: they will abandon me, so I will abandon them. I will abandon them and they will be devoured. God is *predicting* but he is also *waiting*, waiting for the day when the Israelites will act. He is predicting an event that has not *yet* taken place – an event that has still *not taken place* when the *Torah* ends a few pages later. It is an event that remains – to come.

After warning Moses, God tells him for 'now' to write down a 'song' that will act as 'a witness' against the *future* acts of the 'Children of Israel'. With Moses and God, it is always a question of writing. The song first speaks of the past transgressions of the present generation and of God's reaction to these *past* events:

> They slaughtered (offerings) to demons, no-gods . . .
> The Rock that birthed you, you neglected . . .
> When YHWH saw, he spurned (you),
> From the vexation of his sons and daughters.
> He said: I will conceal my face from them,
> I will see what is their future. (32:17–20)

It ends with another prediction for the future:

> But YHWH will judge (in favour of) his people,
> Regarding his servants he will relent. (32:36)

In the *Torah*, the concealing of God's face (*hastarat panim*), the withdrawal and absence of God, is what will come *and* what has already come. On the one hand, it has not yet come. It remains a prediction of abandonment, a terrible warning, a suspended sentence. On the other hand, it has already happened. The Israelites abandoned God, God abandoned them and *then* relented. Is this warning of a future abandonment *absolute*? Or is this abandonment, which has already happened, just another in a *series* of God's oscillations between abandoning *and* relenting?

In this last song of the *Torah*, God opens the wound and heals the wound: 'I myself bring-death, bestow-life, I wound and I myself heal' (32:39). This echoes the remarkable passage of 30:11–19, where God sets out before the Israelites 'life and good, and death and ill' and, while encouraging them to 'choose life', leaves the *choice* to them. God gives life: the rest is up to you. The *Torah* leaves open the question of the *duration* of God's abandonment. Between life and death, on the one hand, there *could* be a thousand abandonments and relentings; everyday, in the constant *oscillation* between losing and regaining faith (*ehmuna*), God opens and closes the wound, abandons and relents. On the other hand, there *could also* be an infinite, catastrophic, never-ending abandonment that is always waiting to happen, that will happen one day, a gaping opening that, still today, even today, has never been closed.

In his commentary on *Deuteronomy* 31:17–18 in *The Guide for the Perplexed*, Maimonides says there are three possible states for man in relation to Divine Providence: sunshine (when we are perfect in our knowledge of God and meditate on God); cloudy (when we have perfect knowledge of God but meditate on other, 'worldly' matters); and, darkness (when we have no knowledge of God) (388–89 [III:LI]). Divine Providence diminishes or departs according to the knowledge of and attention given to God. For those who have this knowledge and remarkable capacity for attention, 'the absence of Providence' is mitigated by the potential to return their attention to God. For Maimonides, it is this oscillation *between* distraction and attention that accounts for 'the ordinary evils [that] befall a prophet or a perfect and pious man'. It is all a matter of the 'duration' of distraction. It is, he insists, 'impossible that any kind of evil should befall him [a perfect and pious man] while he is with God, and God with him'. If there is separation from God, 'we ourselves are the cause of this hiding of the face' and 'the screen that separates us from God is of our own creation'. If we are 'abandoned to destruction like cattle' Maimonides concludes, it is due to 'our separation from God'. God's absence is *entirely* a matter of human action and creation: it has nothing to do with God. God is always there: it is we who *abandon* him. We have made the gap.

Yosl Rakover Talks to God, a fictional account by Zvi Kolitz of the last hours of a Jew in the Warsaw Ghetto uprising of 1943, depicts a mad world that has inverted the order of Maimonides. The sun has become a 'calamity', a 'searchlight' for the Nazis hunting Jews in the woods and it is 'only the night, that concealed us in her heart' (5). It is almost as if when 'God has hidden his face from the world' the sun (the knowledge of and attention to God for Maimonides) becomes deadly and 'only the night' (the hidden and unknown God) offers a perilous chance of life by concealing 'us in her heart'. When God has 'hidden his face from the world' we can only survive by hiding in the absence of God.

For Yosl Rakover, 'when God has hidden his face from the world', he has 'delivered mankind over to its own savage urges and instincts' (4). Mankind, not God, 'has borne . . . and raised' Hitler (4). Without check or restraint – without the face of God – mankind devours itself, always beginning with the Jews. Yosl's faith in the veiled God is undiminished. The hiding of God's face is not the absence of an *absent* God. Yosl's faith is unchanged, but now that God has hidden his face, now that the Jews are 'abandoned to destruction like cattle', Yosl is no longer in debt *to* God. God hides his face and is 'greatly' in debt (9). God owes Yosl. The hiding of God's face does not end the relationship with God; it announces the transference of debt from man *to* God.

In debt to Yosl, Yosl rebukes God: 'where are the limits of Your patience?' (19); 'Forgive those who have turned away from You' (19); 'Stop crowning Your greatness by veiling Your face from the scourging of the wretched!' (21). Rebuking and still loving God, Yosl can only turn to the *Torah*: 'I believe in His laws even when I cannot justify His deeds . . . I love Him. But I love His Torah more' (18). The *Torah*, the call for justice *in this world*, is the *only* resource when God has hidden his face.

'Loving the Torah more than God', Lévinas's commentary on *Yosl Rakover Talks to God* was published in 1955 on the twelfth anniversary of the end of the Warsaw uprising. Lévinas begins by asking the oldest of questions: 'What can this suffering of the innocents mean? Is it not proof of a world without God, where only man measures Good and Evil?' (143). The 'most common answer' to this question, he notes, 'would be atheism'. This would also be 'the sanest reaction' for those who see God as the stern but loving father who rewards and punishes his children (143). For Lévinas, neither 'the empty sky' of atheism nor 'consolations of divine presence' are an adequate response to God hiding his face from the world. The hiding of the face of God is not a question of absence *or* presence. In the Warsaw Ghetto, Yosl experiences:

> the certainty of God . . . with a new force, beneath an empty sky. For if he is so alone, it is in order to take upon his shoulders the whole of God's responsibilities. The path that leads to the one God must be walked in part without God. True monotheism is duty bound to answer the legitimate demands of atheism. The adult's God is revealed precisely through the void of the child's heaven. This is the moment when God retires from the world and hides His face. (143)

Monotheism is childhood's end. God (the father) hides his face and his responsibilities are thrown on to the adult. The only path *to* God is the loss *of* God, the loss of an 'infantile' faith (143). 'Only the man who has recognized the hidden God can demand that He show Himself', Lévinas writes (145).

For Lévinas, in a world in which God 'renounces all aids to manifestation' – in the extremity of 1939–1945 – there is only a God who 'appeals instead to the full maturity of the responsible man' (143). Responsibility 'abandons the just man to a justice that has no sense of triumph' (143). It is a responsibility *without* good conscience. Neither simply far nor near, neither merely inside nor outside, neither an absence that has been and always will be absent nor a manifestation of a plenitude or presence of justice in this world, 'this distant God', the God who hides his face, 'comes from within' (143). God appears *only* in our ethical actions towards others: *à-dieu, à l'autre*. We are abandoned by an absent God *to* responsibility.

Lévinas will later write in *Totality and Infinity* (1961), that 'the absolute gap [*le décalage absolu*] of separation which transcendence implies could not be better expressed than by the term creation' (293; 326). Created but *separated*, God has 'created a being capable of seeking or hearing from afar [*de loin*]' ('A religion for adults' 15; 31). As Derrida has suggested, from the moment God *waited to see* what Adam would name the animals, to 'see the power of man in action', humans have always had the *choice* of belief, of good and ill, of life and death, of justice and murder ('The animal that therefore I am' 385–7). Seeking or understanding *from afar* there will always be the possibility of an absolute abandonment and the experience of an unending oscillation between abandoning and relenting, between rebuking God and taking responsibility, between moments of despair and moments of trust.

Writing in the aftermath of the Second World War, it is remarkable that Lévinas is able to find an ethics and a *possibility* of religion in the God who hides his face. At the same time, the separation that makes this ethics and religion possible is always an 'absolute gap [*décalage absolu*]'. This absolute gap is *not* a theological gap, a gap *for* ontology. As Lévinas observes in *Totality and Infinity*:

> This is an essential precision of the notion of transcendence, utilizing no theological notion. What embarrasses the traditional theology, which treats of creation in terms of ontology – God leaving his eternity, in order to create – is incumbent as a first truth in a philosophy that begins with transcendence: nothing could better distinguish totality and separation than the difference [*l'écart*] between eternity and time. (293; 326)

This absolute gap is the gap *of* transcendence. It is the absolute timelag (*le décalage absolu*), the time difference, the difference *of* time *as* the absolutely other, *as* infinity. For Lévinas, this absolute gap is *creation* – without ontology.

But at the same time, when it is a question of the gap *as* creation how can one think of anything else than the gap between the fingers of God and Adam on the ceiling of the Sistine Chapel, of the unbridgeable and absolute gap as the origin and the *resource* of all transcendence? We are always trying to close the gap, and with God most of all.

15 December 2004.   On 11 November I wrote: 'There is, as far as I know, only one work by Derrida with *l'écart* in the title.' Actually, I think all of Derrida's titles are *écarts*. In 1973, the year before the publication of *Glas*, on the threshold of *Glas*, in *The Archaeology of the Frivolous* Derrida cites, recites, his title in a note as a phrase in the text (he will later discuss the re-citation of the title in *Parages*): 'The archaeology of the frivolous: is this deviation of genius [*écart de génie*]' (68 n. 11; 49). As he notes thirty years later in *Genèse, généalogies, genres et le génie* (2003), genius is also a question of birth, of beginning, of starting, of starting with the gaps (81). The frivolous, he writes in 1973, is an *écart du génie*:

> This frivolity does not accidently befall the sign. Frivolity is its congenital breach: its *entame* [*first cut*], *arché*, beginning, commandment, its putting in motion and in order – if at least, deviating from itself [*s'y écartant*], frivolity, the sign's disposability, can never be or present *itself*. Since its structure of deviation [*d'écart*] prohibits frivolity from being or having an origin [*d'être ou d'avoir une origine*], frivolity defies all archaeology, it condemns it, we would say, to frivolity. (118–19; 103)

Gaps, gaping: the impossibility, *from the start*, of 'being or having an origin'. What else can a title be than an *écart*? What else can a title be than the first cut, the start that can only start by deviating from itself (*s'y écartant*)?

Today, in Blackwell's I saw the new *Oxford Literary Review*, *Angles on Derrida: Jacques Derrida and Anglophone Literature*, edited by Thomas Dutoit and Philippe Romanski. At the end of a short, eloquent tribute to Derrida, the editors quote from *Béliers – Le dialogue ininterrompu: entre deux infinis, le poème* (2003): 'the experience that I call disseminal undergoes and shoulders . . . the test of an interruption, of a caesura or of an ellipsis, of an inaugural cut [*une entame*]' (54). This passage is followed by a sentence that, once again, evokes the gap (*la béance*) that I started with on 12 October in the last paragraph of Derrida's 1959 paper ' "Genesis and structure" and phenomenology' and the question for the '*transcendental I . . .* of its own death [*de sa propre mort*]' as 'opening itself, the gap [*l'ouverture elle–même, la béance*]'. On *5 February 2003* in Heidelberg, speaking of

Hans-Georg Gadamer, who had just died, and of Paul Celan who, always too soon, had died in 1970, Derrida said:

> Such an opening [*béance*] belongs neither to meaning, nor to phenomena, nor to truth but renders them possible in their *restance*, it marks in the poem the hiatus of a wound [*le hiatus d'une blessure*] whose edges [*lèvres*] never close or reassemble themselves. These lips [*lèvres*] form around a speaking mouth which, even when it keeps silent, calls to the other without condition, in the language of a hospitality which can no longer be determined. (54)

The opening that marks a wound that cannot be closed, that 'calls to the other without condition': the impossible mourning *of* Jacques Derrida. After *8–9 October 2004*, it is always the impossible demand of this double genitive. It 'gapes wide open [*klafft es weit auseinander*]', as Celan had written ('Engführung', *Selected Poems* 121–3).

16 December 2004.   'Now even if this faithfulness still sometimes takes the form of unfaithfulness and deviation [*l'écart*] one *must* be faithful to these differences, that is to say, continue the discussion' ('Je suis en guerre contre moi-même' 12). In his "last" interview on *19 August 2004* in *Le Monde*, Derrida speaks of his *(in)fidélité*, his (dis)loyalty, his (un)faithfulness to the dead. With the dead, there is always an *écart*. I cannot avoid *Chaque fois unique* (*The Work of Mourning*), but how does one read this book after the death of Jacques Derrida?

Start with the gaps.

In 'Lyotard and *us*' (1999), written after the death of Jean-François Lyotard in 1998, Derrida quotes from a short text by Lyotard, 'Notes du Traducteur', written for a 1990 issue of the *Revue philosophique de la France et de l'étranger* devoted to Derrida. This short and elliptical text is an example of Lyotard and Derrida using an informal and indeterminate *tu* in their writings (on occasions when they responded to each other's work), while they had always used the formal *vous* in their discussions and conversations. For Lyotard, there is a relation between writing, the *tu* and what appears to be a *suspension* of mourning. Lyotard writes:

> There shall be no mourning [*Il n'y aura pas de deuil*] . . . you make me cry, I cry after you [*après toi*] . . . It is not for this supposed loss that I cry, but for and after your presence [*ta présence à toi*], language [*la langue*], never deserted. Which will always have happened [*eu lieu*] as long as I write [*tandis que j'aurais écrit*],

out of place [*hors lieu*]. This gap gives place and time for tears [*Cet écart donne place et temps aux larmes*]. (233; 280, trans. modified)

Lyotard appears to be responding to the difference (the gap) between speech (*la langue*) and writing in Derrida's work. I (which might be Lyotard) am crying because of the loss of your voice (which might be Derrida's voice), of the presence of you, as you (*tu*). This strange presence (*tu*), will always 'have happened [*eu lieu*] . . . out of place [*hors lieu*] . . . as long as I write [*tandis que j'aurais écrit*]'. The *tu* is a question of writing, because when *we* speak it is always with a *vous*. As long as I write, the strange presence of *tu* has a place, *outside* place. Writing *tu*: a strange presence that is already outside, already an absence, and perhaps already beyond both presence *and* absence.

The gap (*écart*) marks the strange presence of *tu* in writing, as writing *after tu*, after the loss of *tu*. It is a gap that 'gives place and time to tears'. The gap (of writing, in writing) that marks the *tu* that will 'have happened [*eu lieu*] . . . out of place [*hors lieu*]', *gives* place *and* time to tears (*larmes*). Lyotard touches on a sense of writing that is perhaps most apparent when one reads the writing of someone who has just died, as I did when I started writing on *12 October 2004*, the day of Jacques Derrida's funeral – but this is what writing always does. It opens the gap, the tears of the gap.

A few sentences later in the passage that Derrida quotes, Lyotard goes on to write:

> . . . As I write, you [*tu*] do me wrong and I forgive you [*je te pardonne*], but it will never be proven, not even by my tears. As you [*tu*] haunt my writing, without holiness asking anything, I do you wrong [*je te fais tort*]. Do you forgive me? [*Est-ce que te me pardonnes?*] Who will prove it? Mute . . . That is why there is this gap [*il y a cet écart*], "melancholy," a wrong exceeding declared forgiveness, consuming and consummating itself in writing, of which you [*tu*] have no need. That is why mourning is never lifted [*levé*], the fire never put out. (233; 280)

Lyotard appears to suggest that the tears of the gap are not enough: there is always the mute complexity of the inescapable dispute that is out of phase, of the *différend*, of the gap *of* and *as* the *différend*, of the interminable disproportion of the wrong and of forgiveness. *There is always more than one gap*. There are two gaps: the gap of tears *and* the gap of the *différend*. The first declares 'there shall be no mourning' and the second insists 'mourning is never lifted'. The first gap *could* imply that when it is a matter of the strange presence of the *tu* outside of place, in writing, there shall be no mourning (for presence, for the voice, for the subject, *vous*). The second gap *could* imply that the *différend* ensures there can be no *Aufhebung* of mourning.

Derrida responds to this passage from Lyotard (and I have only quoted a few fragments of it) by writing, 'I still do not know how to interpret these words' (334). This impossibility, this impasse – of more than one gap – 'bespeaks the very destiny or fate of mourning' (334). There is always more than one gap: an impossible mourning.

Mourning must be impossible. We cannot assume that we can merely resurrect or interiorize 'within us the image, idol, or ideal of the other who is dead'. Nor can we assume that 'the other who is dead' is simply outside of us and that we are 'a subjectivity that is closed upon itself or even identical to itself' (*Mémoires – for Paul de Man* 6, 21). Mourning is impossible, and for *us* most of all. The 'trace of the other', the other who has died and that remains *other*, is at once inside and outside of us, marking a gap that *moves* in "us", as "us" – the living who sign our name (29, 34–8, 49). Mourning has always already begun. It begins with the name, with naming and with writing the date, with dating: *Jacques Derrida 15 July 1930 – 8–9 October 2004.*

Most of the gaps in *Chaque fois unique* are the gaps of *others*, the gap, the *trace* of the other who has died (Max Loreau: 'Letter to Francine Loreau' 101–2; Louis Marin: 'By force of mourning' 150; Jean-François Lyotard: 'Lyotard and *us*' 233). At the same time, there are so few gaps. It is the danger of the relation between *the* gap and mourning (*the* gap of writing that effaces mourning, *the* gap of mourning that closes itself) that perhaps prompts Derrida's caution. *The* gap of death, of separation, or even as death, if such a thing is possible, can always be crossed. We are always trying to cross the gap. *Écarts* – always in the plural, always the noun *and* the verb, *écart(er)* – the gaps that move, that wander, that cannot be crossed, are always more *and* less than "*the* gap *of* death".

As far as I am aware (and it so easy to miss a gap), from 1981 to 2003 there is only one other scene of the gap in *Chaque fois unique*. On *23 November 1991* at the beginning of his paper on Michel Foucault, who had died in 1984, ' "To do justice to Freud": The history of madness in the age of psychoanalysis', Derrida remarks:

> While accepting wholeheartedly this generous invitation, I nonetheless declined [*écarté*] the suggestion that came along with it to return to the

discussion that began some twenty-eight years ago. I declined [*je l'ai écartée*] for numerous reasons, the first being that one that I just mentioned: one does not carry on a stormy discussion after the other has departed [*après le départ de l'autre*]. (81; 110)

One can add *decline* to the many possible translations of *écarter*. It is significant that Derrida does not use *refuser*, *décliner*, *rejeter* here. He has not refused or declined the invitation: he has accepted 'wholeheartedly this generous invitation [*tout en répondant oui, de grand coeur, à une généreuse invitation*]', he has responded *yes*. He has said yes and '*néanmoins écarté*', nonetheless stepped back from, moved away from, withdrawn from, stepped aside from the suggestion to return (*revenir*) to the arguments that started in 1963 with his paper on Foucault, 'Cogito and the history of madness'. Having responded *yes*, Derrida still withdraws from or pushes aside this return. *Je l'ai écartée*, he explains, because, first of all, 'one does not carry on a stormy discussion after the other has departed [*après le départ de l'autre*]'. But also because, *après le départ de l'autre*, after one has said *yes* to speaking of the other, there are *only écarts* – only '*l'ouverture elle–même, la béance*', '*le décalage horaire*' – that *move away* or *step aside*, that always *pre-cede* me, that mark my first response *to* 'the other who is dead'.

Écarts: the beginning of mourning – for myself, for the other, for Jacques Derrida.

Écarts: the ruins of monu-memorialization. There (are) only gaps and any encyclopaedia of the gaps, of the gaps of Jacques Derrida, can only *fail*, can only encounter the secrets of the gaps, the resistance of the gaps that move: 'no, so long as I do not give to be seen [*je ne donne pas à voir*] and heard the detail of each of the transgressions [*écarts*], and I'll never do so, each of those that your curiosity wants to see, know, archive' ('Circumfession' 103; 99). There (are) only gaps, the gap that Jacques Derrida has left behind him *and* in front of him: the gaps that pre-cede, that go before and go on ahead and that I can only respond to by saying *yes*. There (are) only gaps: *yes*.

'If it does not help me to love life even more, it will have failed [*s'il ne m'aide pas à aimer plus encore la vie, il aura échoué*]' (77; 76).

17 December 2004.   'All this is possible only in the gap [*l'écart*] that separates the text from itself', Derrida writes in the fourth and last gap of *La dissémination* (356; 433). It is Friday afternoon, a crescent moon in the clear, dark winter sky. Ten weeks ago today, sometime between Friday and Saturday, Jacques Derrida died.

Three dreams.

In the first, sometime in October, I came to a waiting room with a few people in it and was greeted warmly by Derrida. We spent a few hours talking. Later, he saw me to the bus station. I got on a bus and asked, 'How do I get to Oxford from here?'

In the second, last night, I was in Derrida's house with a few other people. Derrida spoke to me for a few minutes and then sat down and began to write on a blank piece of paper. Derrida and his wife had been very hospitable. But I knew that he did not have much time and that I should go. I began to gather my books. I awoke before the moment I had been avoiding, the moment, at the door, of saying goodbye.

As if by reading and writing, I could avoid saying goodbye.

I still have only watched the first five minutes of the film *Derrida*. I will watch it, soon.

How does Hegel get to Plato? By leaping (and falling) from gap to gap: *écarts*.

As if all of this was a prefatory aside (*à l'écart préfacier*) to *Glas*.

'The following night I dream that while travelling I learn of my father's death (you know he has been dead since 1970 and that *Glas* is not unrelated to that bereavement). I can't bring myself to believe it – or not to doubt it' (*8 May 1998, Counterpath* 279).

And then it just stops,
and never stops,
stopping

Bibliography

———. *The Five Books of Moses*, trans. Everett Fox (New York: Schocken, 1992).

Aeschylus, *Agamemnon*, in *The Oresteian Trilogy*, trans. Philip Vellacott (London: Penguin, 1986).

Agnon, S. Y., *Shira*, trans. Zeva Shapiro, afterword Robert Alter (Syracuse: Syracuse University Press, 1996).

Althusser, Louis, 'Du contenu dans la pensée de G. W. F. Hegel', in *Écrits philosophiques et politiques*, textes réunis et présentés par François Matheron, 2 vols (Paris: Stock/Imec, 1994), I: 59–238.

Argyros, Ellen, *'Without Any Check of Proud Reserve': Sympathy and its Limits in George Eliot's Novels* (London: Peter Lang, 2000).

Aristotle, *Poetics*, in *The Complete Works of Aristotle*, ed. Jonathan Barnes, 2 vols (Princeton: Princeton University Press, 1984), I.

Aristotle, *Politics*, in *The Complete Works of Aristotle*, ed. Jonathan Barnes, 2 vols (Princeton: Princeton University Press, 1984), I.

Aristotle, *Rhetoric*, in *The Complete Works of Aristotle*, ed. Jonathan Barnes, 2 vols (Princeton: Princeton University Press, 1984), I.

Auerbach, Erich, *Mimesis: The Representation of Reality in Western Literature*, trans. Willard R. Trask (Princeton: Princeton University Press, 1991).

Austen, Jane, *Fragment of a Novel* [*"Sanditon"*] (Oxford: Clarendon Press, 1925).

Barnes, Jonathan, *Early Greek Philosophers* (London: Penguin, 1987).

Beckett, Samuel, *Murphy* (London: Calder, 1993).

Beerbohm, Max, *Zuleika Dobson*, intro. N. John Hall (New Haven: Yale Nota Bene, 2002).

Benjamin, Walter, 'Franz Kafka: On the tenth anniversary of his death', in *Illuminations: Essays and Reflections*, ed. Hannah Arendt, trans. Harry Zohn (New York: Schocken, 1985), pp. 111–40.

Benjamin, Walter, *The Origin of German Tragic Drama*, intro. George Steiner, trans. John Osborne (London: Verso, 1994).

Benjamin, Walter, 'Theses on the philosophy of history', in *Illuminations: Essays and Reflections*, ed. Hannah Arendt, trans. Harry Zohn (New York: Schocken, 1985), pp. 253–64.

Benjamin, Walter, 'What is epic theatre?', in *Illuminations: Essays and Reflections*, ed. Hannah Arendt, trans. Harry Zohn (New York: Schocken, 1985), pp. 147–54.

Bennet, Andrew and Nicholas Royle, *Elizabeth Bowen and the Dissolution of the Novel: Still Lives* (London: St Martins, 1995).

Bennington, Geoffrey, 'Derrida's Mallarmé', in *Interrupting Derrida* (London: Routledge, 2000), pp. 47–58.

Bennington, Geoffrey, 'Mosaic fragment: If Derrida were an Egyptian . . .', in *Derrida: A Critical Reader*, ed. David Wood (Oxford: Blackwell, 1992), pp. 97–119.

Bennington, Geoff and Robert Young, 'Introduction: Posing the question', in *Post Structuralism and the Question of History*, ed. Derek Attridge, Geoff Bennington and Robert Young (Cambridge: Cambridge University Press, 1987), pp. 1–11.

Bialik, Hayim Nahman and Yehoshua Hana Ravnitzky, *The Book of Legends – Sefer Ha-Aggadah: Legends from the Talmud and Midrash*, trans. William G. Braude (New York: Schocken, 1992).

Birnbaum, Jean, 'Jacques Derrida 1930–2004', Cahier du 'Monde', *Le Monde* (no. 18572), 12 October 2004: i–x.

Blake, William, *The Complete Poetry and Prose of William Blake*, ed. David V. Erdman, comm. Harold Bloom (New York: Anchor Books, 1988).

Blanchot, Maurice, 'From dread to language', in *The Gaze of Orpheus and Other Literary Essays*, ed. P. Adams Sitney, trans. Lydia Davis (New York: Station Hill, 1981), pp. 3–20; 'De l'angoisse au langage', in *Faux Pas* (Paris: Gallimard, 1987), pp. 9–23.

Blanchot, Maurice, *The Space of Literature*, trans. Ann Smock (Lincoln: University of Nebraska Press, 1989); *L'espace littéraire* (Paris: Gallimard, 1991).

Bloch, Marc, *The Historian's Craft*, trans. Peter Putnam, intro. Joseph R. Strayer (Manchester: Manchester University Press, 1984); *Apologie pour l'histoire ou Métier d'historien* (Paris: Armand Clin, 1949).

Bowen, Elizabeth, *The Death of the Heart* (London: Vintage, 1998).

Brecht, Bertolt, *Brecht on Theatre: The Development of an Aesthetic*, ed. and trans. John Willett (London: Methuen, 1978).

Browning, Robert, *The Poems, Volume One*, ed. John Pettigrew and Thomas J. Collins (London: Penguin, 1981).

Bulgakov, Mikhail, *The Master and Margarita*, trans. Michael Glenny (London: Collins Harvill, 1988).

Carroll, Lewis, *Alice's Adventures in Wonderland* (London: Penguin, 1946).

Celan, Paul, *Selected Poems and Prose*, trans. John Felstiner (New York: Norton, 2001).

Cervantes, Miguel de, *Don Quixote*, trans. Charles Jarvis, intro. E. C. Riley (Oxford: Oxford University Press, 1998).

Cicero, *De Legibus*, trans. Clinton Walker Keyes (London: Heinemann, 1928).

Cixous, Hélène, 'Ce corps étranjuif', in *Judéités: Questions pour Jacques Derrida*, sous la direction de Joseph Cohen et Raphael Zagury-Orly (Paris: Galilée, 2003), pp. 59–83.

Coleridge, Samuel Taylor, *Collected Letters of Samuel Taylor Coleridge*, ed. Earl Leslie Griggs, 6 vols (Oxford: Oxford University Press, 1956–1973).

Coleridge, Samuel Taylor, *The Complete Poems*, ed. William Keach (London: Penguin, 1997).

Deleuze, Gilles, *Nietzsche and Philosophy*, trans. Hugh Tomlinson (London: Athlone, 1986); *Nietzsche et la philosophie* (Paris: Presses Universitaires de France, 1962).

Derrida, Jacques, 'Abraham, l'autre', in *Judéités: Questions pour Jacques Derrida*, sous la direction de Joseph Cohen et Raphael Zagury-Orly (Paris: Galilée, 2003), pp. 11–42.

Derrida, Jacques, *Adieu: To Emmanuel Levinas*, trans. Anne Pascale-Brault and Michael Naas (Stanford: Stanford University Press, 1999); *Adieu – à Emmanuel Lévinas* (Paris: Galilée, 1997).

Derrida, Jacques, 'The age of Hegel', in *Eyes of the University: The Right to Philosophy 2*, trans. Susan Winnett (Stanford: Stanford University Press, 2005), pp. 117–49; 'L'âge de Hegel', in *Du droit à la philosophie* (Paris: Galilée, 1990), pp. 181–227.

Derrida, Jacques, 'The animal that therefore I am (more to follow)', trans. David Wills, *Critical Inquiry* 28 (2002): 369–418; 'L'Animal Que Donc Je Suis (à Suivre)', in *L'animal autobiographique: Autour de Jacques Derrida*, sous la direction de Marie-Louise Mallet (Paris: Galilée, 1999), pp. 251–301.

Derrida, Jacques, 'Aphorism countertime', in *Acts of Literature*, trans. Nicholas Royle, ed. Derek Attridge (London: Routledge, 1992), pp. 414–33; 'L'aphorisme à contretemps', in *Psyché: Inventions de l'autre* (Paris: Galilée, 1987), pp. 519–33.

Derrida, Jacques, *Aporias: Dying – awaiting (one another at) the "limits of truth"*, trans. Thomas Dutoit (Stanford: Stanford University Press, 1993); *Apories: Mourir – s'attendre aux "limites de la vérité"* (Paris: Galilée, 1996).

Derrida, Jacques, *The Archaeology of the Frivolous: Reading Condillac*, trans. John P. Leavey (Pittsburgh: Duquesne University Press, 1980); *L'archéologie du frivole: lire Condillac* (Paris: Denoël/Gonthier, 1976).

Derrida, Jacques, *Archive Fever: A Freudian Impression*, trans. Eric Prenowitz (Chicago: University of Chicago Press, 1996); *Mal d'Archive: une impression freudienne* (Paris: Galilée, 1995).

Derrida, Jacques, *Artaud le Moma: Interjections d'appel* (Paris: Galilée, 2002).

Derrida, Jacques, 'At this very moment in this work here I am', in *Re-Reading Lévinas*, trans. Ruben Berezdivin, ed. Robert Bernasconi and Simon Critchley (Bloomington: Indiana University Press, 1991), pp. 11–48; 'En ce moment même dans cet ouvrage me voici', in *Psyché: Inventions de l'autre* (Paris: Galilée, 1987), pp. 159–202.

Derrida, Jacques and Antoine Spire, *Au-delà des apparences* (Latresne: Le Bord de l'eau, 2002); to be published in *Paper Machine*, trans. Rachel Bowlby (Stanford: Stanford University Press, 2005).

Derrida, Jacques, *Béliers – Le dialogue ininterrompu: entre deux infinis, le poème* (Paris: Galilée, 2003); to be published in *Sovereignties in Question*, ed. Jacques Derrida, Thomas Dutoit and Outi Pasanen (New York: Fordham University Press, 2005).

Derrida, Jacques, 'Between two throws of dice', an unpublished text cited in fragments in the footnotes of 'The double session', in *Dissemination*, trans. Barbara Johnson (Chicago: University of Chicago Press, 1981), pp. 186–7 n. 14; 'Entre deux coups de dés', cited in 'La double séance', in *La dissémination* (Paris: Seuil, 2001), pp. 228–30 n. 8.

Derrida, Jacques, 'By force of mourning', in *The Work of Mourning*, trans. Anne Pascale-Brault and Michael Naas (Chicago: University of Chicago Press, 2001), pp. 139–64; 'À force de deuil', in *Chaque fois unique, la fin du monde*, présenté par Pascale-Anne Brault et Michael Naas (Paris: Galilée, 2003), pp. 177–204.

Derrida, Jacques, 'Cartouches', in *The Truth in Painting*, trans. Geoff Bennington and Ian McLeod (Chicago: University of Chicago Press, 1987), pp. 183–247; 'Cartouches', in *La vérité en peinture* (Paris: Flammarion, 1978), pp. 211–90.

Derrida, Jacques, *Chaque fois unique, la fin du monde*, présenté par Pascale-Anne Brault et Michael Naas (Paris: Galilée, 2003); *The Work of Mourning*, trans. Anne Pascale-Brault and Michael Naas (Chicago: University of Chicago Press, 2001).

Derrida, Jacques, 'Circumfession', in *Jacques Derrida*, trans. Geoffrey Bennington (Chicago: University of Chicago Press, 1993); 'Circonfession', in *Jacques Derrida* (Paris: Seuil, 1991).

Derrida, Jacques, 'Cogito and the history of madness', in *Writing and Difference*, trans. Alan Bass (Chicago: University of Chicago Press, 1989), pp. 31–63; 'Cogito et histoire de la folie', in *L'écriture et la différence* (Paris: Seuil, 2001), pp. 51–98.

Derrida, Jacques and Catherine Malabou, *Counterpath: Travelling with Jacques Derrida*, trans. David Wills (Stanford: Stanford University Press, 2004); *Le Contre-allée* (Paris: La Quinzaine littéraire-Louis Vuitton, 1997).

Derrida, Jacques, 'The deconstruction of actuality', in *Negotiations: Interventions and Interviews 1971–2001*, trans. Elizabeth Rottenberg (Stanford: Stanford University Press, 2002), pp. 85–116.

Derrida, Jacques, *Demeure: Fiction and Testimony*, trans. Elizabeth Rottenberg (Stanford: Stanford University Press, 2000); *Demeure – Maurice Blanchot* (Paris: Galilée, 1998).

Derrida, Jacques, 'Différance', in *Margins of Philosophy*, trans. Alan Bass (Chicago:

University of Chicago Press, 1990), pp. 3–27; 'La différance', in *Marges – de la philosophie* (Paris: Minuit, 2003), pp. 1–29.

Derrida, Jacques, *Dissemination*, trans. Barbara Johnson (Chicago: University of Chicago Press, 1981); *La dissémination* (Paris: Seuil, 2001).

Derrida, Jacques, 'Dissemination', in *Dissemination*, trans. Barbara Johnson (Chicago: University of Chicago Press, 1981), pp. 287–366; 'La Dissémination', in *La dissémination* (Paris: Seuil, 2001), pp. 349–445.

Derrida, Jacques, 'The double session', in *Dissemination*, trans. Barbara Johnson (Chicago: University of Chicago Press, 1981), pp. 173–285; 'La double séance', in *La dissémination* (Paris: Seuil, 2001), pp. 199–317.

Derrida, Jacques, 'D'un texte à l'écart', *Les temps modernes* 284 (1970): 1546–52.

Derrida, Jacques and Bernard Stiegler, *Echographies of Television: Filmed Interviews*, trans. Jennifer Bajorek (Cambridge: Polity, 2002); *Échographies – de la télévision: Entretiens filmés avec Bernard Stiegler* (Paris: Galilée, 1996).

Derrida, Jacques, 'Edmond Jabès and the question of the book', in *Writing and Difference*, trans. Alan Bass (Chicago: University of Chicago Press, 1989), pp. 64–78; 'Edmond Jabès et la question du livre', in *L'écriture et la différence* (Paris: Seuil, 2001), pp. 99–118.

Derrida, Jacques, *Edmund Husserl's Origin of Geometry: An Introduction*, trans. John P. Leavey (Lincoln: University of Nebraska Press, 1989); *Edmund Husserl, L'origine de la géométrie, Introduction et traduction* (Paris: Presses Universitaires de France, 1974).

Derrida, Jacques, 'The ends of man', in *Margins of Philosophy*, trans. Alan Bass (Chicago: University of Chicago Press, 1990), pp. 109–36; 'Les fins de l'homme', in *Marges – de la philosophie* (Paris: Minuit, 2003), pp. 129–66.

Derrida, Jacques, 'Envois', in *The Post Card: From Socrates to Freud and Beyond*, trans. Alan Bass (Chicago: University of Chicago Press, 1987), pp. 3–256; 'Envois', in *La carte postale: de Socrate à Freud et au-delà* (Paris: Aubier Flammarion, 2003), pp. 5–273.

Derrida, Jacques, 'Et cetera . . . (and so on, und so weiter, and so forth, et ainsi de suite, und so überall, etc.)', in *Deconstructions: A User's Guide*, ed. Nicholas Royle, trans. Geoffrey Bennington (Basingstoke: Palgrave, 2000), pp. 282–305; 'Et cetera . . . (and so on, und so weiter, and so forth, et ainsi de suite, und so überall, etc.)', in *Derrida, Cahiers de l'Herne 83*, ed. Marie-Louise and Ginette Michaud (Paris: L'Herne, 2004), pp. 21–34.

Derrida, Jacques, 'The eyes of language: The abyss and the volcano', in *Acts of Religion*, trans. Gil Andijar (London: Routledge, 2002), pp. 189–227; 'Les yeux de la langue', in *Derrida, Cahiers de l'Herne 83*, ed. Marie-Louise and Ginette Michaud (Paris: L'Herne, 2004), pp. 473–93.

Derrida, Jacques, *Eyes of the University: The Right to Philosophy 2*, trans. Jan Plug (Stanford: Stanford University Press, 2005); second volume of *Du droit à la philosophie* (Paris: Galilée, 1990).

Derrida, Jacques, *Fichus: Discours de Francfort* (Paris: Galilée, 2002); to be published in *Paper Machine*, trans. Rachel Bowlby (Stanford: Stanford University Press, 2005).

Derrida, Jacques and Elisabeth Roudinesco, *For What Tomorrow . . . Dialogue*, trans. Jeff Fort (Stanford: Stanford University Press, 2004); *De quoi demain . . . Dialogue* (Paris: Fayard/Galilée, 2001).

Derrida, Jacques, ' "Genesis and structure" and phenomenology', in *Writing and Difference*, trans. Alan Bass (Chicago: University of Chicago Press, 1989), pp. 154–68; ' "Genèse et structure" et la phénomenologie', in *L'écriture et la différence* (Paris: Seuil, 2001), pp. 409–28.

Derrida, Jacques, *Genèse, généalogies, genres et le génie: Les secrets de l'archive* (Paris: Galilée, 2003); to be published as *Genius, Genealogies, Genres and the Genie*, trans. Beverly Bie Brahic (Edinburgh: Edinburgh University Press, 2005).

Derrida, Jacques, *The Gift of Death*, trans. David Wills (Chicago: Chicago University Press, 1995); *Donner la mort* (Paris: Galilée, 1999). The expanded French edition includes 'La littérature au secret: Une filiation impossible', pp. 163–209.

Derrida, Jacques, *Glas*, trans. John P. Leavey Jr and Richard Rand (Lincoln: University of Nebraska Press, 1990); *Glas* (Paris: Galilée, 1995).

Derrida, Jacques, 'Hostpitality', in *Acts of Religion*, trans. Gil Anidjar (London: Routledge, 2002), pp. 356–71.

Derrida, Jacques, 'If there is cause for translation I: Philosophy in its national language (towards a "licterature en François")', in *Eyes of the University: The Right to Philosophy 2*, trans. Sylvia Söderlind (Stanford: Stanford University Press, 2005), pp. 1–19; 'S'il y a lieu de traduire I: La philosophie dans sa langue nationale (vers une "licterature en françois")', in *Du droit à la philosophie* (Paris: Galilée, 1990), pp. 283–309.

Derrida, Jacques, 'If there is cause for translation II: Decartes' romances, or the economy of words', in *Eyes of the University: The Right to Philosophy 2*, trans. Rebecca Coma (Stanford: Stanford University Press, 2005), pp. 20–42; 'S'il y a lieu de traduire II: Les romans de Descartes ou l'économie des mots', in *Du droit à la philosophie* (Paris: Galilée, 1990), pp. 311–41.

Derrida, Jacques, 'I'm going to have to wander all alone', in *The Work of Mourning*, trans. Anne Pascale-Brault and Michael Naas (Chicago: University of Chicago Press, 2001), pp. 189–95; 'Il me faudra errer tout seul', in *Chaque fois unique, la fin du monde*, présenté par Pascale-Anne Brault et Michael Naas (Paris: Galilée, 2003), pp. 235–8.

Derrida, Jacques, 'Istrice 2. Ick bünn all hier', in *Points . . . Interviews, 1974–1994*, ed. Elisabeth Weber, trans. Peggy Kamuf (Stanford: Stanford University Press, 1995), pp. 300–26; 'Istrice 2. Ick bünn all hier', in *Points de suspension: Entretiens*, choisis et présentés par Elisabeth Weber (Paris: Galilée, 1992), pp. 309–36.

Derrida, Jacques, 'Ja, or the *faux-bond* II', in *Points . . . Interviews 1974–1994*, ed. Elisabeth Weber, trans. Peggy Kamuf (Stanford: Stanford University Press, 1995), pp. 30–77; 'Ja, ou le faux-bond', in *Points de suspension: Entretiens*, choisis et présentés par Elisabeth Weber (Paris: Galilée, 1992), pp. 37–81.

Derrida, Jacques, 'Je suis en guerre contre moi-même', in *Le Monde* Jeudi 19 Août, 2004: 12–13; republished in 'Jacques Derrida 1930–2004', Cahier du "Monde", *Le Monde* (no. 18572), 12 October 2004: vi-vii; and in *Apprendre à vivre: Entretien avec Jean Birnbaum* (Paris: Galilée, 2005).

Derrida, Jacques, 'Justices', trans. Peggy Kamuf, *Critical Inquiry* 31 (Spring 2005): 689–721.

Derrida, Jacques, '*Khōra*', in *On the Name*, ed. Thomas Dutoit, trans. Ian McLeod (Stanford: Stanford University Press, 1995), pp. 87–127; *Khōra* (Paris: Galilée, 1993).

Derrida, Jacques, 'The law of genre', *Critical Inquiry* 7 (1980): 55–81; 'La loi du genre', in *Parages*, novelle édition revue et augmentée (Paris: Galilée, 2003), pp. 231–66.

Derrida, Jacques, 'Letter to Francine Loreau', in *The Work of Mourning*, trans. Anne Pascale-Brault and Michael Naas (Chicago: University of Chicago Press, 2001), pp. 91–103; 'Lettre à Francine Loreau', in *Chaque fois unique, la fin du monde*, présenté par Pascale-Anne Brault et Michael Naas (Paris: Galilée, 2003), pp. 123–34.

Derrida, Jacques, 'La littérature au secret: Une filiation impossible', in *Donner la mort* (Paris: Galilée, 1999), pp. 163–209.

Derrida, Jacques, 'LIVING ON. Border lines', in *Deconstruction and Criticism*, trans. James Hulbert (New York: Continuum, 1979), pp. 75–176; 'Survivre', in *Parages*, nouvelle édition revue et augmentée (Paris: Galilée, 2003), pp. 109–203.

Derrida, Jacques, 'Lyotard and *us*', in *The Work of Mourning*, trans. Anne Pascale-Brault and Michael Naas (Chicago: University of Chicago Press, 2001), pp. 211–41; 'Lyotard et *nous*', in *Chaque fois unique, la fin du monde*, présenté par Pascale-Anne Brault et Michael Naas (Paris: Galilée, 2003), pp. 259–89.

Derrida, Jacques, *Margins of Philosophy*, trans. Alan Bass (Chicago: University of Chicago Press, 1990); *Marges – de la philosophie* (Paris: Minuit, 2003).

Derrida, Jacques, *Memoirs of the Blind: The Self-Portrait and Other Ruins*, trans. Pascale-Anne Brault and Michael Naas (Chicago: University of Chicago Press, 1993); *Mémoires d'aveugle: L'autoportrait et autres ruines* (Paris: Réunion des musées nationaux, 1990).

Derrida, Jacques, *Mémoires – for Paul de Man*, trans. Cecile Lindsay, Jonathan Culler and Eduardo Cadava (New York: Columbia University Press, 1989); *Mémories – pour Paul de Man* (Paris: Galilée, 1988).

Derrida, Jacques, *Monolingualism of the Other; or, the Prothestic Origin*, trans. Patrick Menash (Stanford: Stanford University Press, 1998); *Le monolinguisme de l'autre, ou la prothèse d'origine* (Paris: Galilée, 1996).

Derrida, Jacques, *Of Grammatology*, trans. Gayatri Chakravorty Spivak (Baltimore: Johns Hopkins University Press, 1990); *De la grammatologie* (Paris: Minuit, 1967).

Derrida, Jacques, *Of Hospitality, Anne Dufourmantelle invites Jacques Derrida to Respond*, trans. Rachel Bowlby (Stanford: Stanford University Press, 2000); *De l'hospitalité, Anne Dufourmantelle invite Jacques Derrida à répondre* (Paris: Calman-Lévy, 1997).

Derrida, Jacques, *Of Spirit: Heidegger and the Question*, trans. Geoffrey Bennington and Rachel Bowlby (Chicago: University of Chicago Press, 1989); 'De l'esprit', in *Heidegger et la question* (Paris: Champs/Flammarion, 1990), pp. 9–143.

Derrida, Jacques, 'On cosmopolitanism', in *On Cosmpolitanism and Forgiveness*, trans. Mark Dooley (London: Routledge, 2001), pp. 1–24; *Cosmopolites de tous les pays, encore un effort!* (Paris: Galilée, 1997).

Derrida, Jacques, '*Ousia* and *Grammē*: Note on a note from *Being and Time*', in *Margins of Philosophy*, trans. Alan Bass (Chicago: University of Chicago Press, 1990), pp. 29–68; '*Ousia* et *Grammē*: note sur une note de *Sein und Zeit*', in *Marges – de la philosophie* (Paris: Minuit, 2003), pp. 31–78.

Derrida, Jacques, 'Outwork, prefacing', in *Dissemination*, trans. Barbara Johnson (Chicago: University of Chicago Press, 1988), pp. 1–59; 'Hors livre: préfaces', in *La dissémination* (Paris: Seuil, 2001), pp. 7–68.

Derrida, Jacques, *Parages*, nouvelle édition revue et augmentée (Paris: Galilée, 2003); the first edition appeared in 1986 and the new edition includes ' "Maurice Blanchot est mort" ', pp. 267–300.

Derrida, Jacques, 'La Parole: Donner, nommer, appeler', in *Ricoeur, Cahiers de l'Herne 81* (Paris: l'Herne, 2004), pp. 19–25.

Derrida, Jacques, 'Pas', in *Parages*, nouvelle édition revue et augmentée (Paris: Galilée, 2003), pp. 19–108.

Derrida, Jacques, 'Passions: "An oblique offering" ', in *On the Name*, ed. Thomas Dutoit, trans. David Wood (Stanford: Stanford University Press, 1995), pp. 3–31; *Passions* (Paris: Galilée, 1993).

Derrida, Jacques, 'The pit and the pyramid: Introduction to Hegel's semiology', in *Margins of Philosophy*, trans. Alan Bass (Chicago: University of Chicago Press, 1990), pp. 69–108; 'Le puits et la pyramide: introduction à la sémiologie de Hegel', in *Marges – de la philosohie* (Paris: Minuit, 2003), pp. 79–128.

Derrida, Jacques, 'Plato's pharmacy', in *Dissemination*, trans. Barbara Johnson (Chicago: University of Chicago Press, 1981), pp. 61–171; 'La pharmacie de Platon', in *La dissémination* (Paris: Seuil, 2001), pp. 69–167.

Derrida, Jacques, 'Poétique et politique de témoignage', in *Derrida, Cahiers de l'Herne 83*, ed. Marie-Louise and Ginette Michaud (Paris: L'Herne, 2004), pp. 521–39; to be published in *Sovereignties in Question*, ed. Jacques Derrida, Thomas Dutoit and Outi Pasanen (New York: Fordham University Press, 2005).

Derrida, Jacques, *Politics of Friendship*, trans. George Collins (London: Routledge, 1997); *Politiques de l'amitié* (Paris: Galilée, 1994).

Derrida, Jacques, *Positions*, trans. Alan Bass (Chicago: University of Chicago Press, 1981); *Positions* (Paris: Minuit, 1972).

Derrida, Jacques, *The Post Card: From Socrates to Freud and Beyond*, trans. Alan Bass (Chicago: University of Chicago Press, 1987); *La carte postale: de Socrate à Freud et au-delà* (Paris: Aubier Flammarion, 2003).

Derrida, Jacques, *The Problem of Genesis in Husserl's Philosophy*, trans. Marian Hobson (Chicago: University of Chicago Press, 2003); *Le problème de la genèse dans la philosophie de Husserl* (Paris: Presses Universitaires de France, 1990).

Derrida, Jacques, 'Psyche: Inventions of the other', in *Reading de Man Reading*, trans. Catherine Porter, ed. Lindsay Walters and Wlad Godzich (Minneapolis: University of Minnesota Press, 1989), pp. 25–66; 'Psyché: invention de l'autre', in *Psyché: Inventions de l'autre* (Paris: Galilée, 1987), pp. 11–61.

Derrida, Jacques, 'Qual Quelle: Valéry's sources', in *Margins of Philosophy*, trans. Alan Bass (Chicago: University of Chicago Press, 1990), pp. 273–306; 'Qual Quelle: Les sources de Valéry', in *Marges – de la philosophie* (Paris: Minuit, 2003), pp. 325–63.

Derrida, Jacques, 'The reason of the strongest (are there rogue states?)', in *Rogues: Two Essays on Reason*, trans. Rachel Bowlby (Stanford: Stanford University Press, 2005), pp. 1–114; 'La raison du plus fort (Y a-t-il des États voyous?)', in *Voyous: Deux essais sur la raison* (Paris: Galilée, 2003), pp. 19–161.

Derrida, Jacques, 'Restitutions of the truth in pointing', in *The Truth in Painting*, trans. Geoff Bennington and Ian McLeod (Chicago: University of Chicago Press, 1989), pp. 255–382; 'Restitutions de la vérité en pointure', in *La vérité en peinture* (Paris: Flammarion, 1978), pp. 291–436.

Derrida, Jacques, 'The retrait of metaphor', in *The Derrida Reader*, ed. Julian Wolfreys, trans. F. Gasdner (Edinburgh: Edinburgh University Press, 1998), pp. 102–29; 'Le retrait de la métaphore', in *Psyché: Inventions de l'autre* (Paris: Galilée, 1987), pp. 63–93.

Derrida, Jacques, 'The rhetoric of drugs', in *Points . . . Interviews, 1974–1994*, ed. Elisabeth Weber, trans. Michael Israel (Stanford: Stanford University Press, 1995), pp. 228–54; 'Rhétorique de la drogue', in *Points de suspension: Entretiens*, choisis et présentés par Elisabeth Weber (Paris: Galilée, 1992), pp. 241–67.

Derrida, Jacques, 'Shibboleth: for Paul Celan', in *Wordtraces: Readings of Paul Celan*, ed. Aris Fioretos (Baltimore: Johns Hopkins University Press, 1994), pp. 3–72; *Schibboleth – pour Paul Celan* (Paris: Galilée, 1986).

Derrida, Jacques, 'Signature event context', in *Margins of Philosophy*, trans. Alan Bass (Chicago: University of Chicago Press, 1990), pp. 307–30; 'Signature événement contexte', in *Marges – de la philosophie* (Paris: Minuit, 2003), pp. 365–93.

Derrida, Jacques, *Signéponge/Signsponge*, trans. Richard Rand (New York: Columbia University Press, 1988).

Derrida, Jacques, 'A silkworm of one's own', in *Acts of Religion*, ed. Gil Andijar, trans. Geoffrey Bennington (London: Routledge, 2002), pp. 309–355; 'Un ver à soie', in *Voiles* (Paris: Galilée, 1998), pp. 23–85.

Derrida, Jacques, 'Some statements and truisms about neologisms, newisms, postisms, parasitisms, and other small seismisms', in *The States of "Theory": History, Art and Critical Discourse*, ed. and intro. David Carroll (New York: Columbia University Press, 1990), pp. 63–94.

Derrida, Jacques, *Specters of Marx: The State of the Debt, the Work of Mourning, and the New International*, trans. Peggy Kamuf (London: Routledge, 1994); *Spectres de Marx: L'État de la dette, le travail du deuil et la nouvelle Internationale* (Paris: Galilée, 1993).

Derrida, Jacques, *Speech and Phenomena and Other Essays on Husserl's Theory of Signs*, trans. David B. Allison (Evantson: Northwestern University Press, 1973); *La voix et le phénomène: Introduction au problème du signe dans la phénoménologie de Husserl* (Paris: Presses Universitaires de France, 1993).

Derrida, Jacques, *Spurs: Nietzsche's Styles / Éperons: Les Styles de Nietzsche*, trans. Barabara Harlow, intro. Stefano Agosti (Chicago: University of Chicago Press, 1979).

Derrida, Jacques, *Sur parole: Instantanés philosophiques* (Paris: L'Aube, 1999).

Derrida, Jacques, 'A testimony given . . .', in *Questioning Judaism: Interviews by Elisabeth Weber*, trans. Rachel Bowlby (Stanford: Stanford University Press, 2004), pp. 39–58.

Derrida, Jacques and Derek Attridge, 'This strange institution called literature: An interview with Jacques Derrida', in *Acts of Literature*, ed. Derek Attridge (New York: Routledge, 1992), pp. 33–75.

Derrida, Jacques, 'The time of a thesis: Punctuations', in *Eyes of the University: The Right to Philosophy 2*, trans. Kathleen McLaughlin (Stanford: Stanford University Press, 2005), pp. 113–28; 'Ponctuations: le temps de la thèse', in *Du droit à la philosophie* (Paris: Galilée, 1990), pp. 439–59.

Derrida, Jacques, ' "To do justice to Freud": The history of madness in the age of psychoanalysis", in *The Work of Mourning*, trans. Anne Pascale-Brault and Michael Naas (Chicago: University of Chicago Press, 2001), pp. 77–90; ' "Être juste avec psychoanalysis": l'histoire de la folie à l'âge de la psychanalyse', in *Chaque fois unique, la fin du monde*, présenté par Pascale-Anne Brault et Michael Naas (Paris: Galilée, 2003), pp. 109–20.

Derrida, Jacques, 'To speculate – on "Freud" ', in *The Post Card: From Socrates to Freud and Beyond*, trans. Alan Bass (Chicago: University of Chicago Press, 1987), pp. 257–409; 'Spéculer – sur "Freud" ', in *La carte postale: de Socrate à Freud et au-delà* (Paris: Flammarion, 2003), pp. 275–437.

Derrida, Jacques, *Le toucher, Jean-Luc Nancy* (Paris: Galilée, 2000); to be published as *On Touching – Jean-Luc Nancy*, trans. Christine Irizarry (Stanford: Stanford University Press, 2005).

Derrida, Jacques and Safaa Fathy, *Tourner les mots: Au bord d'un film* (Paris: Galilée/Arte, 2000).

Derrida, Jacques, 'Typewriter ribbon: Limited ink (2)', in *Without Alibi*, trans. Peggy Kamuf (Stanford: Stanford University Press, 2002), pp. 71–160; 'Le ruban de machine à écrire: Limited Ink II', in *Papier Machine* (Paris: Galilée, 2001), pp. 33–147.

Derrida, Jacques, 'Unsealing ("the old new language")', in *Points . . . Interviews, 1974–1994*, ed. Elisabeth Weber, trans. Michael Israel (Stanford: Stanford University Press, 1995), pp. 115–31; 'Desceller ("la vieille neuve langue")', in *Points de suspension: Entretiens*, choisis et présentés par Elisabeth Weber (Paris: Galilée, 1992), pp. 123–40.

Derrida, Jacques and Hélène Cixous, *Veils*, trans. Geoffrey Bennington (Stanford: Stanford University Press, 2001); *Voiles* (Paris: Galilée, 1998).

Derrida, Jacques, 'Violence and metaphysics: An essay on the thought of Emmanuel Levinas', in *Writing and Difference*, trans. Alan Bass (Chicago: University of Chicago Press, 1989), pp. 79–153; 'Violence et métaphysique: Essai sur la pensée d'Emmanuel Levinas', in *L'écriture et la différence* (Paris: Seuil, 2001), pp. 117–228.

Derrida, Jacques, *Voyous: Deux essais sur la raison* (Paris: Galilée, 2003); *Rogues: Two Essays on Reason*, trans. Rachel Bowlby (Stanford: Stanford University Press, 2005).

Derrida, Jacques, 'What is a "relevant" translation?', *Critical Inquiry* 27 (2001): 174–200; 'Qu'est-ce qu'une traduction "relevante"?', in *Derrida, Cahiers de l'Herne 83*, ed. Marie-Louise and Ginette Michaud (Paris: L'Herne, 2004), pp. 561–76.

Derrida, Jacques, 'White mythology: Metaphor in the text of philosophy', in *Margins of Philosophy*, trans. Alan Bass (Chicago: University of Chicago Press, 1990), pp. 207–71; 'La mythologie blanche: la métaphore dans le texte philosophique', in *Marges – de la philosophie* (Paris: Minuit, 2003), pp. 247–324.

Derrida, Jacques, *The Work of Mourning*, trans. Anne Pascale-Brault and Michael Naas (Chicago: University of Chicago Press, 2001); *Chaque fois unique, la fin du monde*, présenté par Pascale-Anne Brault et Michael Naas (Paris: Galilée, 2003). The enlarged French edition includes 'Corona vitae (fragments)' on Gérard Granel (pp. 293–319) and 'À Maurice Blanchot' (pp. 323–32).

Descartes, René, *Discourse on Method*, in *Philosophical Writings*, trans. John Cottingham, Robert Stoothoff and Dugald Murdoch, 2 vols (Cambridge: Cambridge University Press, 1986), I.

Descartes, René, *Meditations on First Philosophy*, in *Philosophical Writings*, trans. John Cottingham, Robert Stoothoff and Dugald Murdoch, 2 vols (Cambridge: Cambridge University Press, 1986), II.

Descartes, *Oeuvres Philosophiques*, ed. Ferdinand Alquié, 2 vols (Paris: Garnier Frères, 1967); *Oeuvres de Descartes*, ed. Adam and Paul Tanney, 11 vols (Paris: Vrin, 1965).

Dick, Kirby and Amy Ziering Kofman, *Derrida* (2002); film directed by Kirby Dick and Amy Kofman (Zeitgeist Films).

During, Lisabeth, 'The concept of dread: Sympathy and ethics in *Daniel Deronda'*, in *Renegotiating Ethics in Literature, Philosophy, and Theory*, ed. Jane Adamson, Richard Freadman and David Parker (Cambridge: Cambridge University Press, 1998), pp. 65–83.

Dutoit, Thomas and Philippe Romanski (eds.), *Angles on Derrida: Jacques Derrida and Anglophone Literature, The Oxford Literary Review* 25 (2003).

Eliot, George, *Middlemarch: A Study of Provincial Life*, ed. Rosemary Ashton (London: Penguin, 1994).

Euripides, *Iphigenia in Aulis*, in *Orestes and Other Plays*, trans. Philip Vellacot (Harmondsworth: Penguin, 1986); *Works*, trans. Arthur S. Way, 4 vols (London: Heinemann, 1966), I.

Finas, L., S. Kofman, R. Laporte and J.-M. Rey, *Écarts: Quatre essais à propos de Jacques Derrida* (Paris: Fayard, 1973).

Fitzgerald, F. Scott, *The Great Gatsby* (London: Penguin, 2000).

Garelli, Jacques, 'L'écart du maintenant et l'extension de l'esprit', *Les temps modernes* 281 (1969): 874–96.

Gaston, Sean, *Derrida and Disinterest* (London: Continuum, 2005).

Gibbon, Edward, *The History of the Decline and Fall of the Roman Empire*, ed. David Womersley, 3 vols (London: Penguin, 1994).

Goethe, Johann Wolfgang von, *Goethe's Faust*, trans. Walter Kaufmann (New York: Anchor, 1990).

Gombrich, E. H., *Art and Illusion: A Study in the Psychology of Pictorial Representation* (London: Phaidon, 1996; 5th edn).

Gowing, Lawrence, *Vermeer* (London: de la Mare, 1997).

Hartog, François, *The Mirror of Herodotus: The Representation of the Other in the Writing of History*, trans. Janet Lloyd (Berkeley: University of California Press, 1988).

Hazlitt, William, 'My first acquaintance with poets', in *Selected Writings*, ed. Jon Cook (Oxford: Oxford University Press, 1998), pp. 211–29.

Hegel, G. W. F., *Lectures on the History of Philosophy I: Greek Philosophy to Plato*, trans. E. S. Haldane, intro. Frederick C. Beister (Lincoln: University of Nebraska Press, 1995); *Vorlesungen über die Geschichte der Philosophie I* (Frankfurt am Main: Suhrkamp, 1986).

Hegel, G. W. F., *Phenomenology of Spirit*, trans. A. V. Miller (Oxford: Oxford University Press, 1977); *Phänomenologie des Geistes* (Frankfurt am Main: Suhrkamp, 1986).

Hegel, G. W. F., *The Philosophy of History*, trans. J. Sibree, intro. C. J. Friedrich (New York: Dover, 1956).

Hegel, G. W. F., *Science of Logic*, trans. A. V. Miller (London: Oxford University Press, 1969).

Heidegger, Martin, 'Anaximander's saying', in *Off the Beaten Track*, ed. and trans. Julian Young and Kenneth Hynes (Cambridge: Cambridge University Press, 2002), pp. 242–81.

Heidegger, Martin, *Being and Time*, trans. John Macquarrie and Edward Robinson (Oxford: Blackwell, 1990); *Sein und Zeit* (Frankfurt am Main: Klostermann, 1977).

Heidegger, Martin, *Identity and Difference*, trans. Joan Stambough (Chicago: University of Chicago Press, 2002).

Herodotus, *The Histories*, trans. Aubrey de Sélincourt and A. R. Burn (London: Penguin, 1972); *The History*, trans. David Grene (Chicago: University of Chicago Press, 1988).

Hobson, Marian, *Jacques Derrida: Opening Lines* (London: Routledge, 1998).

Hoffmann, E. T. A., *The Life and Opinions of the Tomcat Murr*, trans. Anthea Bell, intro. Jeremy Adler (London: Penguin, 1999); *Lebens-Ansichten des Katers Murr* (München: Winkler, 1977).

Hume, David, *A Treatise of Human Nature: Being an Attempt to Introduce the Experimental Method of Reasoning into Moral Subjects*, ed. L. A. Selby-Bigge and P. H. Nidditch (Oxford: Oxford University Press, 1978).

Husserl, Edmund, *Ideas: General Introduction to Pure Phenomenology*, trans. W. R. Boyce Gibson (New York: Collier, 1962).

Husserl, Edmund, *The Origin of Geometry*, in Jacques Derrida, *Edmund Husserl's Origin of Geometry: An Introduction*, trans. David Carr (Lincoln: University of Nebraska Press, 1989), pp. 157–80.

Hyppolite, Jean, *Genesis and Structure of Hegel's Phenomenology of Spirit*, trans. Samuel Cherniak and John Heckman (Evanston: Northwestern University Press, 1989).

Jaffe, Audrey, *Scenes of Sympathy: Identity and Representation in Victorian Fiction* (Ithaca: Cornell University Press, 2000).

James, Henry, *Daisy Miller and Other Stories*, ed. Jean Gooder (Oxford: Oxford University Press, 1985).

Johnson, Samuel, 'Preface', in *Selections from Johnson on Shakespeare*, ed. Bertrand H. Bronson and Jean M. O'Meara (New Haven: Yale University Press, 1987), pp. 8–60.

Joyce, James, *Finnegans Wake*, intro. Seamus Deane (London: Penguin, 1992).

Joyce, James, *Ulysses* (London: Penguin, 1992).

Kant, Immanuel, *The Conflict of Faculties*, in *Religion and Rational Theology*, trans. Mary J. Gregor (Cambridge: Cambridge University Press, 2001), pp. 233–309; *Der Streit der Fakultäten*, in *Schriften zur Anthropologie Geschichtsphilosophie Politik und Pädagogik* (Frankfurt am Main: Im Insel, 1964).

Kant, Immanuel, *Critique of Pure Reason*, trans. Paul Guyer (Cambridge: Cambridge

University Press, 1998); *Kritik der Reinen Vernunft* (Frankfurt am Main: Im Insel, 1964).

Kierkegaard, Søren, *Fear and Trembling / Repetition*, ed. and trans. Howard V. Hong and Edna H. Hong (Princeton: Princeton University Press, 1983).

Kojève, Alexandre, *Introduction to the Reading of Hegel: Lectures on the Phenomenology of Spirit*, ed. Raymond Queneau and Allan Bloom, trans. James H. Nichols (Ithaca: Cornell University Press, 1991).

Kolitz, Zvi, *Yosl Rakover Talks to God*, trans. Carol Brown Janeway, ed. Paul Badde, afterwords by Emmanuel Lévinas and Leon Wieseltier (New York: Vintage, 2001).

Lévinas, Emmanuel, 'Loving the Torah more than God', in *Difficult Freedom: Essays on Judaism*, trans. Seán Hand (Baltimore: Johns Hopkins University Press, 1997), pp. 142–5.

Lévinas, Emmanuel, *Otherwise than Being or Beyond Essence*, trans. Alphonso Lingis (Pittsburgh: Duquesne University Press, 2000).

Lévinas, Emmanuel, 'A religion for adults', in *Difficult Freedom: Essays on Judaism*, trans. Seán Hand (Baltimore: Johns Hopkins University Press, 1997), pp. 11–23.

Lévinas, Emmanuel, *Totality and Infinity: An Essay on Exteriority*, trans. Alphonso Lingis (Pittsburgh: Duquesne University Press, 1996); *Totalité et Infini: Essai sur l'extériorite* (Paris: Le Livre de Poche, 2001).

Lévinas, Emmanuel, 'The trace of the other', in *Deconstruction in Context: Literature and Philosophy*, ed. Mark C. Taylor, trans. A. Lingus (Chicago: University of Chicago Press, 1986), pp. 345–59; 'La trace de l'autre', in *En découvrant, l'existence avec Husserl et Heidegger* (3rd edn.; Paris: Vrin, 2001), pp. 261–82.

Lyotard, Jean-François, *The Differend: Phases in Dispute*, trans. Georges Van Den Abbeele (Minneapolis: University of Minnesota Press, 1988).

Lyotard, Jean-François, 'Notes du traducteur', *Revue philosophique de la France et de l'étranger* 115: 2 (1990): 269–92.

Maggiori, Robert, 'Derrida: l'homme déconstruit', *Libération* 11 October 2004 (no. 7283): 1–7.

Maimonides, Moses, *The Guide for the Perplexed*, trans. M. Friedländer (New York: Dover, 1956).

Malabou, Catherine, 'The parting of the ways: Drift, arrival, catastrophe', in *Counterpath: Travelling with Jacques Derrida*, trans. David Wills (Stanford: Stanford University Press, 2004); 'L'Écartment des voies: derive, arrive, catastrophe', in *Le Contre-allée* (Paris: La Quinzaine littéraire-Louis Vuitton, 1997).

Márquez, Gabriel García, *One Hundred Years of Solitude*, trans. Gregory Rabassa (New York: Harper, 1991).

Melville, Hermann, *Moby-Dick or, The Whale*, intro. Andrew Delbanco, comm. Tom Qurik (London: Penguin, 1992).

Miller, Hillis J., *On Literature* (London: Routledge, 2002).

Milton, John, *Poetical Works*, ed. Douglas Bush (London: Oxford University Press, 1966).

Momigliano, Arnaldo, *The Development of Greek Biography* (Cambridge, MA: Harvard University Press, 1971).

Momigliano, Arnaldo, 'How to reconcile Greeks and Trojans', in *On Pagans, Jews, and Christians* (Hanover: Wesleyan University Press, 1987), pp. 264–88.

Momigliano, Arnaldo, 'The place of Herodotus in the history of historiography', in *Studies in Historiography* (New York: Harper Torchbooks, 1966), pp. 127–42.

Montaigne, Michel de, 'How we weep and laugh at the same things', in *The Complete Essays*, trans. M. A. Screech (London: Penguin, 1992), pp. 262–5.

Nehamas, Alexander, 'Pity and fear in the *Rhetoric* and the *Poetics*', in *Essays on Aristotle's Poetics*, ed. Amélie Oksenberg Rorty (Princeton: Princeton University Press, 1992), pp. 291–314.

Nietzsche, Friedrich, *The Birth of Tragedy*, in *Basic Writings of Nietzsche*, trans. Walter Kaufmann (New York: Modern Library, 1968).

Nothomb, Amélie, *Biographie de la faim* (Paris: Albin Michel, 2004).

Ovid, *Metamorphoses*, trans. Mary M. Innes (London: Penguin, 1955).

Oz, Amos, *The Same Sea*, trans. Nicholas de Lange (London: Chatto & Windus, 2001).

Oz, Amos, *A Tale of Love and Darkness*, trans. Nicholas de Lange (London: Chatto & Windus, 2004).

Perec, Georges, *Life A User's Manual: Fictions*, trans. David Bellos (London: Harvill Press, 1996).

Plato, *Cratylus*, in *The Dialogues of Plato*, trans. Benjamin Jowett, 5 vols (Oxford: Clarendon Press, 1892), I; *Plato*, trans. H. N. Fowler (Harvard: Harvard University Press, 1962), IV.

Plato, *Parmenides*, in *The Dialogues of Plato*, trans. Benjamin Jowett, 5 vols (Oxford: Clarendon Press, 1892), IV; *Plato*, trans. H. N. Fowler (Harvard: Harvard University Press, 1962), IV.

Plato, *Phaedo*, in *The Dialogues of Plato*, trans. Benjamin Jowett, 5 vols (Oxford: Clarendon Press, 1892), II; *Plato*, trans. H. N. Fowler (Harvard: Harvard University Press, 1962), I.

Plato, *Phaedrus*, in *The Dialogues of Plato*, trans. Benjamin Jowett, 5 vols (Oxford: Clarendon Press, 1892), I; *Plato*, trans. H. N. Fowler (Harvard: Harvard University Press, 1962), I.

Plato, *Philebus*, in *The Dialogues of Plato*, trans. Benjamin Jowett, 5 vols (Oxford: Clarendon Press, 1892), IV; *Plato*, trans. H. N. Fowler and W. R. M. Lamb (Harvard: Harvard University Press, 1962), VIII.

Plato, *Protagoras*, in *The Dialogues of Plato*, trans. Benjamin Jowett, 5 vols (Oxford: Clarendon Press, 1892), I; *Plato*, trans. W. R. M. Lamb (Harvard: Harvard University Press, 1962), II.

Plato, *Sophist*, in *The Dialogues of Plato*, trans. Benjamin Jowett, 5 vols (Oxford:

Clarendon Press, 1892), IV; *Plato*, trans. H. N. Fowler (Harvard: Harvard University Press, 1962), VII.

Plato, *Theaetetus*, in *The Dialogues of Plato*, trans. Benjamin Jowett, 5 vols (Oxford: Clarendon Press, 1892), IV; *Plato*, trans. H. N. Fowler (Harvard: Harvard University Press, 1962), VII.

Plutarch, *Lysander*, in *The Rise and Fall of Athens: Nine Greek Lives*, trans. Ian Scott Kilvert (London: Penguin, 1960), pp. 287–318.

Plutarch, 'On the malice of Herodotus', in *Moralia*, trans. Lionel Person (London: Heinemann, 1965).

Plutarch, *Pericles*, in *The Rise and Fall of Athens: Nine Greek Lives*, trans. Ian Scott Kilvert (London: Penguin, 1960), pp. 165–206.

Plutarch, *Themistocles*, in *The Rise and Fall of Athens: Nine Greek Lives*, trans. Ian Scott Kilvert (London: Penguin, 1960), pp. 77–108.

Porter, Roy, *Quacks: Fakers and Charlatans in Medicine* (Stroud: Tempus, 2003).

Proust, Marcel, *Remembrance of Things Past* [*The Search for Lost Time*], trans. Scott Moncrieff, 3 vols (London: Penguin, 1989).

Quintillian, *Institutio Oratoria*, trans. H. E. Butler, 4 vols (London: Heinemann, 1969).

Richardson, Samuel, *Pamela; or, Virtue Rewarded*, ed. Peter Sabor, intro. Margaret A. Doody (London: Penguin, 2003).

Ricoeur, Paul, *The Conflict of Interpretations*, ed. Don Ihde (Evanston: Northwestern University Press, 1988).

Ricoeur, Paul, *Time and Narrative III*, trans. Kathleen Blamey and David Pellauer (Chicago: University of Chicago Press, 1990).

Royle, Nicholas, *After Derrida* (Manchester: Manchester University Press, 1995).

Royle, Nicholas, *Jacques Derrida* (London: Routledge, 2003).

Scheler, Max, *The Nature of Sympathy*, trans. Peter Heath, intro. W. Stark (London: Routledge, 1954).

Scholem, Gershom, 'Walter Benjamin', in *On Jews and Judaism in Crisis: Selected Essays*, ed. Werner J. Dannhauser (New York: Schocken, 1976), pp. 172–97.

Shakespeare, William, *The Comical History of the Merchant of Venice, or Otherwise called The Jew of Venice*, in *The Norton Shakespeare, Based on the Oxford Edition*, ed. Stephen Greenblatt and others (New York: Norton, 1997).

Shakespeare, William, *The First Part of the Contention of the Two Famous Houses of York and Lancaster (2 Henry VI)*, in *The Norton Shakespeare, Based on the Oxford Edition*, ed. Stephen Greenblatt and others (New York: Norton, 1997).

Shakespeare, William, *The Tragedy of Hamlet, Prince of Denmark*, in *The Norton Shakespeare, Based on the Oxford Edition*, ed. Stephen Greenblatt and others (New York: Norton, 1997).

Shakespeare, William, *The Tragedy of Julius Caesar*, in *The Norton Shakespeare, Based on the Oxford Edition*, ed. Stephen Greenblatt and others (New York: Norton, 1997).

Shakespeare, William, *The Tragedy of Richard the Third*, in *The Norton Shakespeare, Based on the Oxford Edition*, ed. Stephen Greenblatt and others (New York: Norton, 1997).

Shakespeare, William, *The Winter's Tale*, in *The Norton Shakespeare, Based on the Oxford Edition*, ed. Stephen Greenblatt and others (New York: Norton, 1997).

Shelley, Percy Bysshe, *The Major Works*, ed. Zachary Lender and Michael O'Neill (Oxford: Oxford University Press, 2003).

Smith, Adam, *The Theory of Moral Sentiments*, ed. D. D. Raphael and A. L. Macfie (Indianapolis: Liberty Fund, 1984).

Taplin, Oliver, 'Emotion and meaning in Greek tragedy', in *Oxford Readings in Greek Tragedy*, ed. Erich Segal (Oxford: Oxford University Press, 1983), pp. 1–12.

Whitman, Walt, *Complete Verse, Selected Prose and Letters*, ed. Emory Holloway (London; Nonesuch, 1938).

Wordsworth, William, *Letters of William Wordsworth: A New Selection*, ed. Alan G. Hill (Oxford: Oxford University Press, 1984).

Wordsworth, William, *The Prelude: A Parallel Text*, ed. J. C. Maxwell (London: Penguin, 1988).

Wordsworth, William, *Selected Poems*, ed. Stephen Gill (London: Penguin, 2004).

Zweig, Stefan, *The World of Yesterday* (Lincoln: University of Nebraska Press, 1964).

'Oxford 1942' from **12 December 2004** was first published in *Succour* (Sussex Creative and Critical Writers) 1 (April 2005): 26–33. sussexsuccour@hotmail.com.

Index